Decluttering Mastery

3 Books in 1 - A Step-By-Step Decluttering Workbook, Complete Guide to Declutter and Organize Your Home, and How to Transform Your Life

Lisa Hedberg

© Copyright 2022 - All rights reserved.

The content contained within this book may not be reproduced, duplicated, or transmitted without direct written permission from the author or the publisher.

Under no circumstances will any blame or legal responsibility be held against the publisher, or author, for any damages, reparation, or monetary loss due to the information contained within this book, either directly or indirectly. You are responsible for your own choices, actions, and results.

Legal Notice:

This book is copyright protected. This book is only for personal use. You cannot amend, distribute, sell, use, quote or paraphrase any part, or the content within this book, without the consent of the author or publisher.

Disclaimer Notice:

Please note the information contained within this document is for educational and entertainment purposes only. All effort has been executed to present accurate, up to date, and reliable, complete information. No warranties of any kind are declared or implied. Readers acknowledge that the author is not engaging in the rendering of legal, financial, medical, or professional advice. The content within this book has been derived from various sources. Please consult a licensed professional before attempting any techniques outlined in this book.

By reading this document, the reader agrees that under no circumstances is the author responsible for any losses, direct or indirect, which are incurred as a result of the use of the information contained within this document, including, but not limited to, errors, omissions, or inaccuracies.

Table of Contents

Your Free Gift   v

Decluttering Advice

Introduction	3
1. Why a Home Can Get Cluttered	5
2. The Perks and Traps of Space	18
3. The Sentimental Gatherer	31
4. The Kitchen	41
5. The Bathroom(s)	54
6. Bedrooms	67
7. Common Areas	78
8. Outdoor Space	96
9. Housework Economy	104

Decluttering Workbook

Quote	113
Introduction	115
How to Use This Book	121

Part One
Preparing for the Transformation

1. The Power of Your Self-Image and the Importance of Goal Setting	125
2. Getting Your Vision Crystal Clear	135
3. Your Habits Reveal a Lot About You!	143

Part Two
Getting to the Root of Your Clutter Issues

4. Clutter is Essentially Decisions You Are Procrastinating On	155
5. Your Perfectionism is Keeping You from Living a Neat and Tidy Life	164
6. Habits of a Neat and Tidy Person	173

Part Three
Decluttering for Life

7. Start with YOU!	191
8. Kickstart the Decluttering Process	204
9. How to Stay Motivated While Decluttering and Using Decluttering Checklists	215

Part Four
Mastering the Art of Organizing and Living Clutter-Free

10. How to Organize Your Home and Your Life	229
11. Routines and Checklists	253
12. Pro Tips on Living a Clutter-Free Life	263
Conclusion	269

Decluttering Your Kitchen in 5 Easy Steps

Quote	273
Introduction	275
1. Assessing and Planning	279
2. Decluttering the Kitchen	287
3. Cleaning the Kitchen	297
4. Organizing the Kitchen	307
5. Meal Planning	317
Conclusion	323
Thank You	325
References	327

Your Free Gift

As a way of saying thanks for your purchase, I'm offering the eBook, *7 Tips to Declutter Your Life* and the *Decluttering Workbook* for FREE to my readers.

To get instant access, just go to:
http://publishingdove.com/

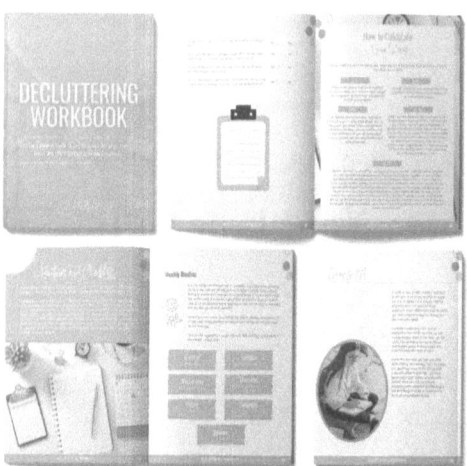

Inside the free download, you will discover:

- A printable format of all the exercises and checklists from the book, *Decluttering Workbook: The Essential Guide to Organize and Declutter Your Home With Exercises and Checklists*

- A colorful, stunning, and eye-catching exercise and checklist design

And you will have the option to write in, cut out, and hang or pin the printable worksheets however you like!

Inside the eBook, you will discover:

- Decluttering tools that will save you hours on decluttering your home.
- The secret decluttering techniques that the experts swear by.
- Authentic views, relatable advice, and a fruitful and wholesome decluttering experience from an author who has been in a similar position as you before.
- How to avoid a messy home and even messier thoughts with this book that will guide you through the journey of decluttering your living space and your life.
- And so much more!

If you want to live a happier, healthier life and look forward to coming home every day, make sure to grab your free eBook.

Decluttering Advice

Easy Ways to Reduce Stress and Declutter Your Home Like a Minimalist

Introduction

The human being is like a sponge. Everything that surrounds them is assimilated in one way or another, which can be both a virtue and a frailty. If the environment we live in is not ideal, this will undoubtedly affect our state of mind, our mood, our productivity, and our deeper emotions.

In no other place is this more evident as in the question of how a family takes care of their house. The most general habit in this regard is, of course, accumulation. Days and weeks and months go by in everybody's lives, but in a house they do not go by in vain. After even the smallest fraction of time, if people aren't alert, stuff will accumulate all over the place.

Does this sound at all familiar to you? That's because we've all been through it. We know it all too well. But how does one get out of this vicious circle? Is there a recipe one can follow? You may be asking these questions fairly regularly, and I believe I have an answer: Decluttering your home like a minimalist.

Introduction

As you will learn throughout this book, it is harder than it seems. This is primarily because it involves being firm against our most ingrained desires and habits. But don't worry. I will walk you through it and give you some of my experiences as I went through the same process. Just remember, there is nothing abnormal about your problem. Many people have been here before, and now it's your turn to get your house in better shape!

Chapter 1

Why a Home Can Get Cluttered

"If you've been feeling frustrated about your house, most likely much of the reason lays here—in the alignment between your possessions and your purposes"

— *Joshua Becker*

Why indeed?

It's a simple question, and simple questions can be the toughest to answer. This comes in part from the fact that no two homes are exactly the same. Although two people can both find themselves submerged in the chaos of their own daily lives, the reasons why each has arrived at that point can be totally different.

For my part, I can tell you I am a family person. We all know how that can lead to a lot of seemingly harmless chaos, don't we? Well, let me tell you about it. I live in Vancouver, British Columbia with my husband and two lovely children, Lily and Quinn. For as long as I can remember, I have found it incredibly difficult to declutter the house and free up some space for the things we like to do as a family. I have had to give up many plans on account of my own inability to set things straight.

It's not that the house posed challenges nobody else has had to face. I'm a financial journalist who has been working from home for the past six months, and as it turns out I was able to witness just how easy the house would get stuffed with things nobody was really using. Because of this, I started to become an obsessive cleaner. Every day that went by seemed impossibly short—and I started to get suffocated by my own stress. I just couldn't find the time to do everything I had to do. Even worse, this pressing feeling inside me started to show. Friends and family alike looked at me and felt worried.

> Are you okay?
> You don't look so well.
> Is anything wrong, Lisa?
> How can we help?

Most of the time I didn't answer. No, sir! I just shook my head and stayed quiet. My own clutter was my own private business, I thought. And boy was I dead wrong about that. The truth is there is no shame in having a cluttered environment. It happens to everyone. As I said, it doesn't always happen the exact same way, but it's something we all have to go through. If people live in a place, it's only natural for that space to get a bit messy every now and then. Well, in all honesty, it can get more than a bit messy. But, that's exactly what we'll go through here.

So, has this happened to you too by any chance?

Decluttering Advice

One day you just find yourself in front of a myriad of things to do, appointments to attend, people to call, errands to run. You say: okay, I can do this. You bravely pick up a pen and start scribbling a list, putting everything in order. Whatever it is you're facing, you manage to do it. But a mere two or three days later everything is upside down again. Not your duties per se, but your home. It's as if this place had turned into a battlefield. Well then, something's going wrong, right?

In the process of venturing into this brave mission you have totally abandoned your own home. You were so busy straightening things up at work that by the time you got back to the errands at home you fell asleep with exhaustion. You wish you hadn't, but you were just too tired and couldn't help it. Then you wake up and realize you're surrounded by a mess that prevents you from thinking clearly—and that gets you really mad, doesn't it?

This is something very common for all those people who do not have the habit of tidying up. Don't get me wrong; no one's judging anybody. What I mean to say is an organized life isn't about raising an arms race against yourself. For all the difficulties you face in doing it, that's just not the right approach. Instead, an organized life is about changing habits and incorporating a new order into life itself. Much easier said than done, right? If I didn't know that already I wouldn't even be here to begin with. Don't worry, I feel you. But give this some time, please. There are no magic solutions, and the first step is always to realize exactly what kind of situation you're in. This is what we'll cover throughout the book.

First, we need to look at the causes of the problem. I will share with you what my own personal methods were to avoid being overcome by a cluttered home. Whether your case is similar or not, in the end you will certainly make your own choices based on what *you* need. Either way, keep in mind that before jumping into action, understanding is key to all solutions.

Procrastination

There is much to be said about the many reasons that can lead to disarray at home, but what about the state of mind that leads to that state of affairs? What does that look like in the first place? In other words, what goes on inside our heads when things get out of control?

Behind actions there is always a train of thought, even if it's just a tiny instinct. A person can often dismiss that inadvertently, while focusing on external factors only. Remember that when you look at a cluttered home, you're looking at the consequences, not at the causes of the problem. The thing is, consequences certainly play a part; they are what sounded the alarm, after all. But the reason they do is connected to something we can only find in ourselves. If we are to recover any control at all, we first need to backtrack a little and see what's what.

One possible outcome from this inward squinting will probably point towards procrastination. A bit of a fancy word, I know, but I guarantee you'll be familiar with the concept even if you didn't hear the word before. To put it simply, it means doing now what you shouldn't do right now and leaving what is most urgent for later. It means having your priorities a little distorted, which over time can be the threshold to having them totally upside down.

The key word here is "nonsense." For someone to procrastinate, there is usually no apparent reason behind it. You should be totally free to do your duties. However, you may find yourself constantly bouncing back to other things. Of course it'd be wrong to underestimate this. On the surface, it seems so gratuitous and easily solvable. Yet that is not always the case. We usually don't realize we procrastinate when we're doing it, and that's because we look everywhere else to find out what's going on, but we forget to look inside ourselves.

Picture the following scenario: You want to check the basement and throw away all the things nobody has used in a long time. The deadline you imposed on yourself for this is looming on the horizon and you know you should start as soon as possible. You're sitting there in front of your inbox, you have a ton of work, and it has been too long since you were able to tell apart your job from your daily life. The perks of remote work, huh? You desperately want to go down there, but there's just no way you're getting up from that desk anytime soon. You're stuck. By the end of the day, you're very, very tired. You feel a little frustrated and resort to looking at some homecraft magazines for comfort. A few minutes go by and you have subscribed to a couple magazines, you've called a friend to tell them about your amazing plans for the basement, and that's it. You didn't even go down there to turn on the lights.

Procrastination is sneaky precisely because it doesn't present itself as an outright waste of time. At first, you feel the urge to do what you have to do, but then all of a sudden you start getting distracted all too easily, albeit for good reason, but still. You think to yourself: *This isn't what I intended to do, is it? Well, it seems important anyway.* Once you're done, you look to the side and realize you haven't cleaned up your house again. You had such great plans about reorganizing spaces and making it all look nice, but somehow you went astray.

When it doesn't seem possible to keep on the wrong track, you remember to call your mother and ask how she's been doing. The two of you end up talking for an hour or two. By now you really *are* distracted from your plans, and perhaps not for the best of reasons anymore. In fact, you've missed your deadline by a lot. Then when you look up to the window, you see the sun isn't there anymore. A cold feeling starts to climb up through your spine and you get worried. Your entire expression freezes in a kind of panicky grimace. You've just wasted a whole afternoon.

What just happened? There was no good reason to avoid sinking your teeth into this project. There is also no way of saying that all the things you did do are in any way inherently wrong. No, this isn't about that. It's about timing. What is more, it's about focusing on whatever you can find to keep delaying that daunting project a little longer. In the end, it is therefore about not being able to confront a particular challenge, perhaps because you're overworked, out of laziness, or perhaps because you're worried what the outcome will be. Either way, you do other errands in order to get distracted from your main goal—turning the basement into a cozy place for the family to hang out.

People who suffer from this problem are basically just pushing the can further down the road. Since this will not make things disappear, what happens is, later on, you'll have much less time to take care of them. On top of that, the place looks awful because the project you had is still nothing but a dream. Hence the stress and the frustration.

Multitasking

Not everybody procrastinates, though. Many people are pretty capable of looking at their to-do list and organizing their priorities accordingly. Not because they're "better" than those who do suffer from the previous problem, but because everyone's different. Remember what I said at the beginning? As seen from the outside, two houses in disarray can look pretty similar. Once we get a closer look, though, we have a very different story to tell. So don't worry, this isn't a competition. It's a matter of distinguishing between different forms of the problem, so as to be able to think of appropriate solutions for each one.

Okay then. What happens when you don't find it difficult to focus on cleaning up the home, but rather have far too many responsibilities, each as important and as urgent, so you simply cannot take care of the house the way you'd like to? This is a pretty common problem for people who work from home; or have to travel great distances in their commute; or simply have no one to share their errands with. I call it the superhero dilemma and it's basically about how a cluttered lifestyle often leads to a cluttered home, because there simply isn't enough time to think about it. In cases like this you'd like to think about the home, but at the end of each day you're just not up for it. In this case you're getting detoured against your will.

Now, this is a tough nut to crack. We all like to live in a pleasant place that reflects our caring and imagination, but there are limits to our energy when we have other things to do too. If we are to find order in our home, we can't afford to ignore those limits. They actually need to be at the center of our agenda. That's why multitasking is good and even vital up to a point, until it degenerates into a superhero dilemma. If you find yourself in a similar situation, the best thing you can do is split the goal into smaller pieces and avoid getting impatient in the meantime. If you're consistent, then decluttering the home will take longer than usual, but it will happen.

It all comes down to learning how to multitask properly. As we all know, perhaps nowadays more than ever before, our busy and demanding lifestyles push us to do several things at the same time. It happens both at work and at home. We answer the phone while we put our papers (and our ideas) in order. We cook while we help our children with their homework. Sometimes, we even take on this unnatural tendency to combine actions to the point of absurdity, as when we believe we are able to call people or send text messages on the phone while driving. Has any of this ever happened to you?

It is not for nothing that the ability to multitask is something that is often sought after when companies look to hire a new employee. Indeed many companies value their employees with a "multitasking profile" ranking. And when we're asked, we ourselves highlight among our talents the ability to do more than one thing at a time. The point is that being a proficient multitasker has come to be a standard of modern life. It isn't a merit anymore; it's actually expected that we have this ability.

This is when things go wrong because in order to keep up with expectations, we push ourselves beyond our limits. We promise to handle a zillion things all at once and pretty soon start running in circles, unable to handle so much as one thing properly. The point is that being a multitasker is not the same as being versatile or having a great power of concentration. These latter aptitudes can be considered a virtue in most cases, but only as long as they involve alternating tasks as opposed to doing them all simultaneously. The same goes for when you're trying to make room in a hectic schedule behind the scenes. Think, for example, of Mrs. Doubtfire. Do you know the movie? That poor lady had to go through a lot in order to keep things looking nice and neat.

Numerous neuroscientific studies, for example Hallowell (2006), have shown that the ability to multitask is probably nothing more than a myth. I know. It sounds crazy, right? Well, these studies hold that the human brain is not equipped to handle more than one single task at a time; at best, it can switch rapidly between one task and another. And even that comes at a cost. Even when we try to shift our attention to common, everyday tasks, like moving a gear lever while driving, it takes us longer to complete them when we're doing something else on top of that. This happens because brain activity suffers in the transition period, and as a result we lose mental agility in the short term. As I said, the classical example of this is using a phone while driving.

So, is multitasking really a myth?

The short answer is that it probably doesn't need to be. The problem is that we often overestimate our own capabilities. It is one thing to be able to hold a conversation while crossing the street or reading a book while making sure we don't miss our subway stop. But going from there to trying to balance our accounting in excel while working through a zillion other tabs on our browser and overlooking our children, all at the same time... Well, let's just say no one's really benefiting from those juggling ventures. Not you, not your children, not your accounting—and most importantly, not your home either. In other words, doing too many things at once amounts to doing none of them. In that case, you might as well just take a break and *really* do nothing for a couple minutes. At least that way you'll get some rest.

The reality is that we are far more cognitively limited than we like to admit. Handling various things properly means putting them in order and focusing on one at a time, one after the other. If you want to apply this principle to your home, that means splitting big goals into smaller pieces. You might not be able to clean up the basement in one single round, but if you do it little by little, you can eventually get it done.

Overcomplicating

This is the problem I used to have. It took me some time to realize it too. At first I just told myself I didn't have time to look back because I had too much to do. This led me to believe I had all the answers beforehand, so there was no point in evaluating different methods to undertake the many things we wanted to change at our house. That was a mistake. In retrospect, I could have saved a lot of time and effort by choosing the right strategy before acting, and listening to other people's advice. If I didn't do that back then, once again this was because my own state of mind prevented me from doing any constructive self-criticism. In other words, trouble didn't come from the outside. It was all in my head.

Answering the question of why we overcomplicate our existence is not an easy feat, nor is it finding a way to avoid doing it once we've realized we have this problem. Personality traits are stable tendencies in the way we act in certain circumstances, which help predict our behavior in specific situations. Thus, for example, people with a high degree of anxiety, with difficulties for decision making and with an inclination to negativity, tend to show this in the way their personal space looks. They tell themselves: "I have no other option," but what they don't realize is they themselves are closing the door on all other options.

This kind of behavior can turn really dangerous once we start enjoying ourselves in difficult times. The way a home is arranged can have a real impact on the way we feel, so when that space is constantly cluttered, that changes our mood. We can normalize it over time and start thinking all shambles are normal. But how easy could life be if we chose to simplify it instead?

People who do not know how to simplify tend to take the most labyrinthine path possible, simply because they have not been willing to accept the shortcut. Sometimes, this happens because we want to give special care to how we organize our home, so without us noticing we confuse care with impracticality.

As with everything else, overcoming this problem is first of all about addressing a slightly drifted state of mind. Then when we're able to appreciate the benefits of a simpler path, at least at a purely theoretical level, it's all a question of training ourselves to adopt that path in every new situation. For example, do you feel you want to put more plants in a room and give it a little life? That's a great idea. Just make sure you don't get carried away and buy a whole army of plants right away. Instead, try to start simple. Why not buy just a couple of small plants and see how that works for starters? Then after a week of having given this a fair trial period, you can decide whether you want more or not.

The principle of practicality has perhaps been most elegantly stated by David Dunham in his book *The Silent Land* (2016).

There he said that "efficiency is nothing more nor less than intelligent laziness." In the context of making our home fit our expectations, this means taking small steps and giving ourselves a chance to taste before we decide. Oftentimes what makes domestic work a burden is the fact we do things too quickly. We go to great lengths to see things better, and then if we don't like the result, we're too tired to take this with a good attitude. You must understand that housework is precisely that: work. If you overcomplicate it, it will be unpleasant. And if you are able to solve things in a simple, intelligent manner, this doesn't make you any less worthy of merit and self-pride. On the contrary, it gives you the energy you need to do the work with care and pleasure.

In Closing

I want to give this a comprehensive scope, which is why I didn't target any specific types of methods just yet. Procrastination, multitasking, and overcomplicating are much more than that. They are three of the broad traits that can be found at the heart of most cluttered homes. Sometimes, we can even encounter combinations of more than one of these traits in a single case. The possibilities are probably infinite, so there is no point in trying to look at a textbook approach to your own situation. Some books will promise to give you just that, but chances are they won't be able to deliver on that promise.

In order to really grab the bull by the horns, as it were, we need to start very generic. Then as things get more clear and we come to understand the causes behind the problem of a cluttered home, we can gradually narrow down our scope and look straight into the mirror. I'd like you to think of this as a self-exploration voyage. Your house is your personal sanctuary. It's supposed to make you and your family feel safe, comfortable, and happy. But the only way to make this happen is by doing the work of decluttering our home with enjoyment.

Key Takeaways

- As problems go, home clutter is one and the same for everyone, but it can originate and look quite differently from one person to the next.
- The three obstacles we discussed: procrastination, multitasking, and overcomplicating.
- Procrastination works both ways; it means resting when it is resting time and doing housework when it is time to do that as well. Having a clear schedule is the only thing that enables that to happen. Otherwise, you can have many good intentions, but the results will be mostly underwhelming.
- On the same line, doing several things at once is simply going to be a must for us. But we can't do it without order, and again, that order can only come from having a solid schedule and following it with discipline.
- No solution too complex is good. One of the lessons this book intends to give is that minimalist solutions are the best because they solve a problem and they do it efficiently.

Chapter 2
The Perks and Traps of Space

"It has taken me years to figure out what I've always heard is true, that too much of a good thing can turn into a bad thing"

— *Myquillyn Smith*

Let's start by picturing a small room. All houses are, more or less, a complex arrangement of rooms, so if we master this basic unit we can master the whole ensemble too. This is going to be challenging, but it's important you don't get frustrated right away. For many of us, the feeling of having too much stuff can cause panic, but tidying up doesn't mean you should get rid of everything you own. If you get frustrated you might feel tempted to do just that, and it would probably be a mistake.

Why do we make that mistake? I think one of the primary reasons is that we face the problem all on our own. Instead of sharing and taking the time to teach our kids the importance of keeping the house in order, we throw things away without putting too much thought into it. That's just not an ideal solution. Moreover, it sends the wrong message to our kids. As you shall see, I will stress the importance of sharing housework as a family in several parts of the book.

But let's get back on track. Sometimes a small room can give us the feeling that we have to throw everything away, but that is not true. Things are expendable only if we know for sure we won't need them later. Other than that, we can put them on the side and look at the space we have. Recognizing what works for you and what doesn't is something that will come on its own after you've really memorized that room in your head.

Think about what you intend to do in that room. What purpose will it serve? Will it be a studio, a room for the kids to play, a bedroom, a guest room? The implication here is that an empty room is like all other rooms. Only after you fill it up with things will it become different from the rest. That is because it now has a function. But the point is we're not at that stage anymore. All rooms have been filled already, and no, they currently do not have a function. They did before, but they are all cluttered now and it is difficult to tell what they were initially intended for. There are simply a lot of questions to ask yourself before you start decluttering that place.

I think you'll agree with me that the best thing is to sit down and contemplate these small spaces one by one, then take a pencil and paper and fill out a series of questions below. Try to do it conscientiously so you can at least imagine what it was like when you could plan all this stuff from scratch. These questions will allow you to become more aware of what you have and what you need, and that will in turn be the first step in making housecraft decisions. So let's see, what could we put in that list?

- Does it have natural lighting?
- Where are the windows and doors placed in this room?
- How many closets does it have?
- What is their location?
- Do you have more storage space in addition to closets?
- What needs does this room need to fulfill?
- How much are people going to move around in it?
- Is this room intended for someone in particular or is it a common area?

When you think about these questions, remember there is no single solution to any of them. The other thing is once you know a little more about your plans for this room, you should start picking things to throw away, but not everything. There is always a way to fit things in a neat and simple way that allows you to free up space and also avoid getting rid of things you could find useful later. That's why you planned on paper first, to have a little trial and error stage.

Now, I know this can get a little repetitive and boring, especially if you happen to have a huge home with a ton of rooms to cover. That's where our previous multitasking discussion becomes important. You see, you're not obligated to do this in a single round. That seems pretty reasonable, right? But it turns out that as you make progress, this will be particularly difficult to accept because houses have a way of looking even more chaotic precisely when we rearrange them. If it takes you two weeks to finish it all, say, that means you're looking

Decluttering Advice

at two weeks of regular clutter plus organization clutter on top of it. And there are no two ways around it either. You simply must put up with it, knowing that there's a silver line waiting for you in the end.

Things are easier if you have a clear image of what your house looks like inside your head. But regardless of whether you know it by heart or need to take some measures before you start, fill up the same questionnaire for all rooms. When you're done, think of them as files and put them side by side. Try to see how they work together as a team now. Use these files as a kind of blueprint of your house. Not the one you live in right now but the one you intend to have after putting things in order. If you feel you need to, you can even draw some basic plans of each room so as to visualize things better.

Thanks to the fact that so far you haven't moved a thing, an important decision should arise from this without too much effort on your part: exactly how much do you intend to do? And try to be totally open about this. As I said, things get overly cluttered when reorganizing things. The last thing you want is to start a big project and not be able to take it to completion. In fact, if you're new at this, I'd especially recommend you start small as a way to test yourself and the method itself for the first time. For starters, focus on a single room and try not to test this in a place that the family uses very often, so as not to disrupt anyone's daily life.

But back to the question of how much you intend to do. This will give you a time horizon and a general scope of the task you're about to embark on. First merely as a general idea, but then as you fill each room's file with more and more details, this idea will become much more precise. Once you reach this point yourself, you can go to step two of the planning stage.

This time, you need to produce another round of blank sheets of paper. They will be attached to the ones you already have and in this case they'll be filled with a list of specific objects, furniture and whatnot. The goal is to decide what you'll be throwing away and what you'll keep.

I'm sure you will agree that's a very difficult thing to do. I think there are basically two alternatives. You can either throw things away or give some of them to friends or a charity. There are some things we definitely know have no useful value anymore, no matter who we give them to. But there are many other things that a bunch of people might find useful, so there's no point in throwing those away. The key, however, is where to draw the line. Allow me to elaborate on how we can solve this riddle.

Children's clothes are a perfect example. Our kids grow pretty fast during the first few years, so they leave a lot of clothes behind without really having worn them out. It'd be a pity to throw them away because, in some extreme cases, they're almost as good as new. But we don't always know someone who has a kid around the same age, so even though we'd like to give the clothes to someone, we can't. We throw them out for lack of a better alternative.

Of course you could go on Facebook Marketplace, take some photos and put your things on sale. This is a great solution, but it is only an option if you have the time to keep track of orders, customer questions, and shipping. If you don't have spare time to sell your discarded clothes, the next best thing is donating them. Look around your area, ask a few questions and you'll certainly find a good place. Then, it's only a matter of taking stuff there every once in a while. I, for instance, donate clothes, books, and occasionally some electronics.

Decluttering Advice

Finding people who can put this stuff to good use is very rewarding. It helps declutter the house, but it also opens up a new perspective on how wasteful life can be and what we can do to change that.

Now, there are a number of things you're not going to feel so sure about. You can't donate everything and, in fact, some things you do need. You just don't know for sure. In other words, you need a trial period. Personally, I don't think there's only one alternative for this, but the solution I came up with is as follows: there are two levels to discard things. Specifically, you can get a big cardboard box and at first, before you intend to throw them away, you can keep things you're unsure about in this box. Also, try to do it carefully so as to avoid breaking anything because the goal here is to be able to retrieve a thing or two if you change your mind.

After you put what you intended to throw away in that box, you can just go about your days in normal fashion. But here's the trick: pay special attention to whether you miss any of the things you set aside, and if you do, ask yourself how much you miss them. If anything should pass those two tests, whether you miss it and whether you miss it a lot, then bring it back from the box. I call this the "Command-Z Solution" because it basically allows me to undo things just like I would on a computer.

One important reminder: these two steps we were talking about before, filling a questionnaire and a list for each room, are critical for the overall success of your project. In other words, take as much time as you need doing them and try to avoid getting impatient at all costs. It will probably feel as though you haven't made any progress at all, and that's because you haven't. But keep in mind that the very reason you want advice to declutter your home is because previous methods didn't work. It isn't enough to grab some things and tidy up a little every day. I mean, to be clear, it certainly does, but only when there is a solid foundation underneath. That's our real goal here. We're not looking for fleeting solutions that will make things look better for just a while. We want to build a foundation to avoid all sources of clutter in the present as well as the future. And that's why it is very important you take your time with these first steps.

Time to Start

Now that you have a more concrete image of the problem at hand, you can start drafting a master list of things to do. As I said, you can start with a single room, but some lists are indeed much bigger and cover the reorganization of an entire house. Our rule of thumb here is that the size of your project must be determined by the amount of spare time you have and the amount of hands that will be collaborating on the project. Ideally, the whole family can become a sort of ad hoc enterprise for the whole weekend and work as a team. Furthermore, this will give you a pretext to spend some quality time together and away from your daily dose of screen time.

So, where to start?

The first thing in all projects of this nature is to find a place where you can put stuff temporarily while you move things around everywhere else. In other words, you need to find a spare room. And if you can't, you need to come up with one. For example, moving everything to one side in the living room. I reckon this is not ideal but, hey, it worked for me a couple times. Now, if you have a little more luck, you'll have a place in the house that people don't use that much. In my case, it is the garage, since it has room for two cars and we only have one. Some people will even have an actual storage unit on the back of the house. If that place is relatively empty, you're all set, but whatever your situation is, find a place for this purpose. It doesn't need to be nice, it just needs to be practical.

Try to free up as much space as you can in that room because, as I said, that's where you'll be putting stuff from other rooms later. In a way, you'll be playing a tetris of sorts, fitting shapes into one room while you free up space in another. This process will take place over and over for as long as you need, so make sure your spare room (or space) is in a passing area so as not to make very long journeys back and forth. For example, in my case, that means I can't really use my garage because it is too far down the house. Hence the living room solution.

Also, before you move on to the next stage, don't forget to go get a bunch of cardboard boxes. If you're lucky enough to have them already, then all the better. If not, you can always find some at the supermarket or ask your friends. People always have boxes from the things they've purchased, and they are often very keen on getting rid of them somehow. That makes them, and you, a perfect match because you'll need boxes to move things around comfortably.

The Bulky Part of the Job

You can prioritize based on what first triggered your will to declutter your home. For example, it could be that you found the shelves and corners of your home office were starting to become a dump. People now have trouble working there, so why not start there? More often than not, we all need to split the job of organizing our house into a series of sessions. With that in mind, choose the places you first want to tidy up depending on what you most need to become operative and pleasant again.

Next up, get to work. Following the lists that you made, pick up all the stuff you can find in the room you intend to enhance, take it to your spare room and put it in two different groups: one for things that will be thrown away and one for those you will rearrange. Once again, if you're not sure what goes into which group, just use the command-z solution. Chances are you won't be able to move the furniture, at least not the bigger pieces, but either way you should empty all drawers. Remember, this is a makeover. Also, make sure you put important documents in a separate box. If it makes you feel more secure, take that box to your room so there's no risk of mixing it up with all the rest.

Be very mindful as you go about this process and avoid overusing the command-z solution. It is fundamentally an option to undo things, so it requires us to make room for an alternative that will only be useful if and when we retrace our steps. But what if we don't? In that case we'll have wasted room for something we didn't end up using. So, keep this solution close at hand, but also think twice every time you think about using it.

As I call it, this is going to be the bulky part of the job. It requires you to go back and forth, pick up stuff and drop it off elsewhere, repeat the process, until at some point both your body and mind will get a bit fed up. This is why it's important to take on this home project as a team. That way you can chit chat and share a few laughs while moving boxes around,

Decluttering Advice

which will make it a lot more bearable. It is also worth pointing out that all the dust you'll shake off from moving things around will cause a lot of sneezing, perhaps even some irritation or allergy. The thing is there is no point in dusting off before reorganizing, so in order to prevent this from bothering you too much, it is best if you purchase some masks. Since we're coming out of a pandemic, chances are you already have some at home.

Dust is, in fact, a very big problem. If masks aren't enough, I will tell you a neat little trick of mine. Get a spray bottle and fill it up with water, shoot a couple sprays in the room you'll reorganize before you start. Not too much, but enough to cover all surfaces in the room. That will cause all the dust to get mixed up with a zillion minuscule drops of water, which will make dust heavier and prevent it from flying around your face. I can't tell you how much that trick has helped me throughout my own decluttering ventures. I'd have developed respiratory problems by now if it wasn't for it. The beauty is, you don't need to worry about ruining any electronic gadgets because water is sprayed in very small particles. Just don't get carried away and you'll be safe.

Setting Checkpoints

Depending on the size of this first bit, you'll probably be done after a couple of hours. That in itself represents a significant amount of work, and, the thing is, you're not done yet. You've just cleared space for the real work to begin. What matters is you have reached a checkpoint. So again, you don't need to worry if by now you've run out of time or simply feel too tired to continue. Just take your master list, check as many boxes as you were able to complete, and leave the rest for later.

However, an important caveat arises from this last consideration. You see, because life can't simply be stopped on account of your domestic decluttering, you simply must manage to make room for both an ongoing life and the project at home. This means that when you choose which spaces you wish to reorganize first, you also need to take into account two important aspects:

- How soon you need that space to be operational again.
- How long you think it will take you to bring it to that point.

In the case of a home office, for instance, you'll probably need it to be up and running before the start of a new week. If that is the case and you think you won't be able to fix it all up in one single weekend, here's what you can do. Go over the exact same process, but leave half the office as is, making sure you leave in place everything you might need for later. Mind you, this isn't always going to be possible. Sometimes a room is laid out in such a way that you simply can't split the task in half. Then you'll have to buckle up and finish the whole thing by any means necessary. But again, this is where our previous discussion about overcomplicating comes in. The reason I asked you to make so many lists beforehand is because you now have a clear idea of the challenges each individual room involves. Granted, you can't always split a room into two sessions, but it's almost certain you *can* go over each room in a single session. The rooms that require more work are generally going to be common areas, and those are ones you generally do have a chance to split into more than one session.

Do you get where I'm going with this? The idea is simple: Don't take on more than one room at a time. No matter how optimistic you may feel about your ability to do it all in one session, make sure you never cover more than one room at any given time. That way you can work for as long as you can and stop at some point without feeling worried or guilty. Since all other rooms remain untouched, at the very least you will have 90% of the house still usable.

This is so important we should make it a golden rule. If you break it, the worst that can happen is you won't be able to tell apart what you fixed and what you didn't fix. That's really bad. It means you now have to go over all of it again, simply because there is no clear boundary between real progress and clutter. A majority of people have so much to cover when reorganizing their homes that they almost certainly aren't going to be fixing it all quickly. The success of your own decluttering project depends on how good you are at splitting tasks into smaller portions and drawing a clear line between clutter and progress.

Key Takeaways

- Start by establishing the basics: what was a room intended for and what stands in the way of it going back to being functional? If you can do that for one room, you can do it for all of them.
- Space is as much a freedom as it is a liability. Having too much of it can lead to more clutter

instead of helping find a place for all the things we have.
- For a proper makeover, take your time in evaluating each room in the same way I mentioned earlier.
- Find a place where you can put stuff temporarily so as to free up space in the areas you wish to rearrange.
- Prioritize according to what first triggered your urge to declutter.
- If you're not sure about whether to throw something away, use the command-z solution: put things aside and throw them away after you've tested and confirmed you really didn't need them.
- The job will be big and hard. You need to set checkpoints to be realistic about how to undertake the challenge.
- Don't ever do more than one room at a time, even if you're enthused about it. It is better to go slowly and keep a good track of everything than to get carried away.

Chapter 3
The Sentimental Gatherer

"I strongly believe that we need to learn to balance the need for housework with actually living"

— *Gemma Bray*

Ever since I was a kid, I had trouble moving from house to house. It was one thing to be moving things around, books and toys for the most part. But I was fine with that, really. My only problem started when me and my parents moved from a big two-story house in Boston to a tiny little apartment in New York. There wasn't enough room in our new place, so my mother asked me to think very well, take a deep breath and decide what I would be getting rid of. Even as I developed a few techniques for this over the years, I must admit I still find it very difficult to do. That's why I want to discuss it here with you because decluttering a home is not just cumbersome, it's also emotionally hard, and we need to be prepared for it.

Lisa Hedberg

The primary sources for attachment are gifts and things we've had during a memorable experience of some kind. For instance, I once got a wooden photo frame as a gift. It was very nice and the person who gave it to me is someone whose friendship I cherish a lot. However, the size of the frame was weird, so I couldn't ever manage to fit my photos in it. They were either too tall or too wide for the frame, and, of course, I wasn't going to cut a photo just to be able to fit it in there. I have been told cutting a photo shouldn't be that big a deal, but anyway, I personally wouldn't.

I took the frame with me to every house my family and I moved into. Wherever we went, I made sure I made some room for it at my desk, at my bedside table, even in my kitchen. At some point I decided to face the problem: the frame looked nice anywhere I put it, but the only photos I could fit there were far too small for it. They looked so tiny in there they almost looked like a joke of some kind. So with all the pain in my heart I called my friend and told him I couldn't keep the frame because none of my photos fit there. I made it clear that I wasn't suggesting I needed a new gift or anything. I was just being honest because I felt rather guilty about throwing it away. To my surprise, he understood perfectly and said I should give it to someone else.

Now, what is the point I'm trying to make? This sort of thing doesn't seem very threatening on its own, but the problem actually starts a little later. We get one gift of this kind, then another, and another, and pretty soon we're up to our necks with a whole bunch of them. The same thing goes for things we've purchased ourselves; we had nearby during some intimate experience, and now find it very difficult to let go. In both cases, the emotional attachment is, of course, not a negative thing in itself. Yet it stands in our way of reducing the amount of stuff that causes constant clutter in the house. Therefore if we let emotions get too strong, eventually we find that we don't want to throw anything away. If we are going to establish order in the house, we must learn to think with a cooler head.

Having a Filter on Entry

Put simply, we need to learn how to say no. I know it feels wrong and it often hurts people's feelings, but if you're honest and sensible enough, there is nothing you can't say on the line of respect. Moreover, choosing not to say no can get us into trouble. Let's say you receive something and are unable to refuse. Regardless of this, you're going to have to dispose of it sooner or later. If you do and you get caught, that can indeed be offensive to people. Not so much because you weren't able to find space for the gift, but because you weren't honest.

I don't know if you're familiar with the sitcom *Seinfeld*, but in that series they branded people who get rid of gifts behind people's backs as "regifters." This refers to the fact that, if you don't explain your situation and give away the gift as a gift, once again, you're recycling a gift. Of course, that's much worse than simply saying no. So the question is, do you want to be a regifter or do you want to be honest with people?

This principle can be extended to other areas too. We sometimes can't be honest with ourselves either. We go to Walmart and suddenly decide we should buy a new pair of reclining chairs for the lawn. We know this idea is ludicrous because we already have a pair, but we like the chairs or the promo we found so much that we can't resist. Later, when we "find" that we didn't have enough room for a new pair of chairs, we get frustrated because we've added yet more stuff to the clutter we have at home.

Same thing with people who aren't really giving us gifts but actually decluttering their own homes themselves. Has this happened to you? Could be anyone, a friend or relative, calling to ask whether you wouldn't be interested in a secondhand trampoline for your kids. You sit there in silence, certain that it's not a good idea to accept because your lawn is far too small for it. But the kids would love it, you think, and you end up saying exactly the wrong thing: "Alright, I'll take it. Thanks!"

What do all these situations have in common? They teach us that, a lot of the time, clutter can be self-inflicted. It's not that we can't locate it when it turns up. We know very well what it is we had to avoid, we just didn't have the willpower to resist, and now we're paying the price.

To stop this from happening, you must strengthen refusal and also be diplomatic about it, but ultimately firm, both to others as well as yourself. You also need to put this filter right at the door. Once things have entered your home, you can be sure that the battle is lost already. To keep the house in order, you need to intercept things as they arrive. Use that moment to look at them carefully and judge whether you really need them. Be objective about it and avoid all emotional justifications. It doesn't matter if you've always wanted a green porcelain bowl and feel happy that your cousin brought you one. Did you already have a bowl? It doesn't matter what color it is, if the bowl you have is still functional, you should refuse the gift. Your cousin will understand.

Usage Discipline

The key ingredient for this filter to work properly is knowing, not just what you have, but what you use. Sometimes we'll take the bowl our cousin brought for lack of this ingredient. Even though we were determined to refuse excess stuff, the problem is we haven't been tracking our possessions thoroughly enough. In other words, we took the bowl because we were certain we didn't have one, but we were ill informed. When we go back to the kitchen and find out we had a pair already, that means we have a total of three now. We weren't using those bowls so we forgot about them, which begs the question: If we had two bowls forgotten in some drawer, how are we going to find a use for the three we have now?

In the previous chapter, we discussed the command-z solution. Therefore you might be thinking these accidents can happen, but you can always go back a few steps, give away a couple bowls and return to normality. This is no doubt a useful option, but we mustn't forget it is above all a contingency. The name itself makes it explicit. People use command-z on their computers to undo stuff. That means you're acknowledging you made a mistake and wish to fix it. Now, I have no objection to that, which is why I recommended it. Ideally, though, we ought to try to avoid mistakes altogether. We'll certainly make a few here and there, but a lot less than if we rely solely on the command-z solution.

A good example of how to exercise usage discipline is with our shopping habits. For example, let's say you're buying your regular brand of cereal and find that it now has a promotion: for every box that you buy, you get a branded cup as a gift. So you think to yourself: *well, that sounds marvelous. I've always wanted to drink coffee out of a cup that says*

Kellogg's in bright red. And it's free, right? There should be no harm in taking it, even though you can see there are boxes without the promotion a couple of shelves away.

Here's the thing. You probably have a dozen cups of your own, if not more. Moreover, you probably bought a set so that all your cups look the same. So imagine what you would do after buying this cereal box with the promotion. You could have visitors that same day in the afternoon, coming over for tea time. In all honesty, would you use the branded cup with them? I don't think so. It's a question of it being useless. Everyone would have a nice cup, and then all of a sudden some unlucky visitor would be drinking their tea out of a Kellogg's cup. That doesn't look nice, does it? You know why? Because people rarely ever use promotional cups or any gift of that sort. So don't get carried away and try to avoid all forms of acquiring excess stuff.

The other big enemy of usage discipline is the way people are used to classify their domestic tools in hierarchies. Allow me to explain. When we have a full size family and an active social life, we usually have more than one set of tableware. At the very least, we tend to have two sets. We have a fancy set for special occasions, Christmas dinners, Thanksgiving and whatnot, and we also have a regular set for everyday use. Then as time goes by, we, of course, have many more everyday use cases than special occasions. We also develop a sort of paranoia about the fancy set, going to great lengths to make sure it doesn't suffer any damage.

While this is certainly reasonable, especially when the fancy set is very expensive, we must face the bitter truth. Our fancy set is not much more than another example of something we don't have much use for. It's enough for us to get invited to other people's houses over a certain period to find out it's been over a year since we've used the fancy set. We know it's there but haven't even seen it in a long time. It's just sitting there, gathering dust in the dark.

Luckily, this doesn't mean we must get rid of our fancy set of tableware, and the same goes for everything we cherish but use too little around the house. I'm talking about things like a special tablecloth, living room covers, fancy silverware, a luxurious carpet, expensive liquor, even our most elegant clothes. Almost none of these things come to mind when thinking about donations because they're important to us, even if we don't get to use them all that often. So what can you do with them?

My advice is you simply use them without shame. This is what I chose to do after having dusted off a ton of things and never actually using them. Although it may sound a bit cliché, I thought to myself: *well, we only live once, so everything I have and cherish, I should use*. Who's to say having a simple intimate dinner with your family can't be enough of a special occasion to use the fanciest tableware you have? Granted, it may break or tarnish a little as a result of regular usage, but isn't that what things are meant for? I guarantee you clutter is at least 50% due to stuff we wouldn't spread around if we knew what we got them for in the first place.

Attach Your Emotions to People, not to Objects

This leads us to the main lesson of the chapter. Being a sentimental gatherer is fundamentally a problem deriving from how we relate to material objects. Either neglecting them or having too strong an attachment to them, the point is we don't know how to manage our possessions properly. We accumulate them like any normal person would, as a mere product of daily activities, social commitments, and family purchases. Everyone has an understanding of this, but it is just as important such accumulation habits be addressed from the first day with an equally rutinary cleaning and purge.

I know, it sounds harsh, but remember who caused objects to be meaningful in the first place. It is people who accumulate things and not the other way around. So that's ultimately what matters: people.

- Gifts: you can take and give away as many as you want and nothing will change, so long as you keep in contact with the people who gave them to you. That's what matters most.
- Fancy acquisitions: their purpose is primarily special occasions, but they won't ever represent specific memories until we actually use them. And anything can be a special occasion when you're invested in looking at it that way.
- Unused things: no matter where they came from, who gave them to you or how much they cost, the rule is if you can't use them, you shouldn't make room for them either. Having discipline on this is the recipe to prevent all future clutter-generating issues.

This can all sound nice and reasonable, I mean, we can agree with it in principle, but it's much harder in practice. Try to put yourself to the test and see how it goes for you. Look, for example, at an old pair of shoes one of your children used to have when they were just learning to walk. Moreover, look at the clothes and possessions we inherit when a close relative has passed away. It's fine if you want to keep a thing or two as a reminder, but sometimes people leave a veritable ton of things behind them.

I, for instance, inherited a couple thousand books from an old aunt of mine once. As I told you, I'm a financial journalist, so I'm into books. It's not as though knowing I'd be getting my aunt's library made me unhappy. On the contrary, I was jumping up and down about it. The problem is I'm a mother of two children and my house isn't exactly a mansion, so I needed to compromise. And you know what? Once I looked around those books, I found a lot of things I wasn't going to use anyway, like medical books, tourist brochures, and a bunch of Guinness Record books. None of that was useful to me and by donating it I was able to keep a much smaller, useful library that I've been carrying with me since then.

Key Takeaways

- All clutter starts with us. If we can discipline our way of acquiring new things and discarding old ones, then we can move from addressing clutter to preventing it altogether.
- Put a filter at the entrance and be very firm about it. Things cannot or should not enter the home unless they are visibly useful for something.
- Use everything you have. There are things we don't throw away because we really do need them, even though we use them very little. For that to change, you need to use everything you have without shame.

- Don't feel bad about letting some things go. Objects represent memories, but they themselves aren't the carriers of any memory. Keep in touch with people and souvenirs will keep coming and going without much difference.

Chapter 4

The Kitchen

"Let's imagine a cluttered room. It does not get messy all by itself. You, the person who lives in it, are involved too"

— *Marie Kondo*

During the following chapters, we will elaborate on specific techniques you can implement, always building on the foundation of the general method we discussed previously. These techniques are going to be based on the need to focus on different areas of the house and the concrete difficulties each of these areas imply to us. In this sense, I would like to start with the kitchen because it is a place that can affect a number of other areas when it isn't functional and well organized. If you want a house to work like a house, it is simply crucial to have the kitchen up and running as best as possible. As an example, allow me to briefly tell you a little story of mine that will show us exactly how a properly kept kitchen is at the center of any decluttered house.

Lisa Hedberg

At the beginning of our married life, my partner and I were still used to keeping the house as two single people living together. Granted, during our dating period we came back and forth and shared our spaces a lot, but it wasn't until we officially started living together and later got married that we needed to come up with a different approach. This became all the more evident once we had children. The logistics, the timeframes, and the sheer volume of things to do: it all became more difficult and hectic.

Once we took a short trip for the weekend, visiting my parents for Christmas. The whole week, in preparation for this trip, my husband and I went around splitting errands and taking turns to take care of the kids. He would go out for a couple of hours to buy gifts and a bunch of other things my parents had asked us to bring. A little later, when we realized he had forgotten something, I would go out again and buy it. The whole week went by in this way so quickly that we both totally forgot about the kitchen. It was slowly building up into an absolute mess, but we had both been so busy taking care of other stuff that we didn't even realize, and we left for our trip.

When we came back, we saw most of our pots had dried food at the bottom. We had left food residue on almost all the dishes, so an army of ants had come to colonize our kitchen table. In the refrigerator, several products had passed their expiration date and began to give off a bad smell around them. Everything was a mess, and well, the saddest thing of all is that some pots we just couldn't get back to normal. We had to throw them away.

The Kitchen, One of the "Lungs" of the House

In fact, there are two lungs in the house, just like in the human body: the kitchen and the bathroom. These are perhaps the most ordinary places of the house, most of us use them strictly in a functional manner and forget about them the rest of the time. If we pay more attention to them, however, we realize they're the elements that allow all the rest of the house to "breathe," as it were. That's why I call them the "lungs" of the house, because by keeping the kitchen and bathroom clean and tidy, the rest of the house becomes easier to cover. They set the pattern of organization that will govern all other rooms, in a way that is marvelously in tune with the philosophy of this book: simple is best.

There is probably nothing less motivating to start the day with joy and good spirits than entering a kitchen that is always disorganized, full of junk, with the table not clean and clear, the sink always full of dirty pots and pans, the floor strewn with crumbs you feel with your feet as you walk around, and a garbage can that's about to burst with trash like a volcano. That is certainly not a place you would like to be at 7 am when you're about to start your day, is it? Anyone who has to go through that will most definitely adopt a kind of mood throughout the rest of their day, simply on account of this awful beginning they have to go through.

A family's way of life and emotional stability is always indirectly reflected by the way they keep their home clean and organized. This is noticeable from the outside too. Mind you, all order shouldn't ever be a matter of presenting yourself to others, but rather of self-care. The priority is keeping our environment in sync with our positive emotions and avoiding getting used to a cluttered life.

Getting back to breakfast in a dirty kitchen, you might notice how getting used to clutter manifests itself in small things. For example, you'll probably want to have breakfast outside. That way the problem will seem to disappear for a while, but doing this over and over can be expensive. Plus when you get back home at night, that kitchen is still going to look messy. So what can you do?

The first thing is to gather all the supplies and cleaning products you're going to need. For this, because you want to keep things simple, start by looking in your own kitchen. It is very common to find that when a kitchen is disorganized, it contains a million useful things we weren't aware of. Also, you're going to need a big bag or perhaps a box for what you intend to throw away. If you want to take things up a notch, get a bag *and* a box. The bag will be to throw garbage in, while the box will be to put stuff you might want to donate or reuse later.

Okay, so you have all your tools at hand. It's time to get started. As discussed in the previous chapter, decluttering sessions take their fair share of time, so we should split them into smaller portions according to our possibilities. In order to be organized on this, set up a timer on your phone. I usually let it run for 30 minutes, then take a quick five-minute break, and resume for another round of 30 minutes. Now, this is the "power hour session" I like to do on weekends, when I need to go over several different areas around the house. On weekdays, though, I have a shorter timer: I clean up for 10 minutes and that's it. Anything that goes beyond what I can do in that timeframe, I put it on my list and keep it there during the weekend's power hour.

Decluttering Advice

To start this longer session, take a general look at what's ahead of you on that list. You should also review the agenda so as to see what you did on previous weekends as well as what you can save for future ones. You need to get used to the idea that cleaning is an ongoing task: you do what you can each day and you don't get stressed out when you can't finish it all because you have a routine, so you know it will be done the following day.

After reviewing your list, set the timer and start cleaning. Depending on what you have to do this time, you'll be starting a whole new set of tasks, while some other times you'll continue where you left off the day before. There are basically two options in this regard:

- Going left to right.
- Setting priorities.

In the case of going from left to right, you're basically going on autopilot. That's good if you already know what to do and are simply following along. However, depending on what day you're in and the amount of time you have at your disposal, autopilot is not necessarily going to work for you. This is because you run the risk of not finishing everything you started. That's where priorities come into play, specifically the whole list scheme we laid out in the previous chapter. The only thing is that, for this scheme to be functional, a clear distinction must be made between:

- Decluttering a major mess.
- Everyday decluttering.

As you can imagine, a power hour is intended to give you time to undertake major tasks, like the mess I told you about before, when I ended up discarding half my stash of pots after Christmas. In cases like that, you usually need to spend an entire power hour just moving things around, before you do any actual cleaning. We often forget that in order to optimize our energy, we first need to figure out what it is that we have to do. Well, if you can avoid getting anxious, then don't feel bad about spending an entire hour setting up a plan. It's just a strategic move, and the better you do it, the sooner you can move on from decluttering a major mess to regular, everyday decluttering.

With a major mess, you first lay out the plan and then usually take a few sessions more before you actually bring things back to normal. In the case of a kitchen, this usually involves learning how to remove grease from dishes and pots, doing deep cleanings of the oven, the stove, even the dishwasher itself. All the machines you use there need to be kept in good condition so that they don't fail at the least expected moment. In fact, maintenance is an area where you shouldn't only keep machines clean yourself but have them checked by a specialist from time to time. In a way, this also falls into the decluttering category, and you should schedule a call every few months for it.

As for everyday decluttering, these are things you *can* do on autopilot once you've made sure the areas you need to cover. Say, for instance, that your list is more or less like this: sweeping up, putting the groceries in their right place, washing the dishes, throwing out the garbage, and checking whether any product is about to expire. I personally would say 10 minutes aren't enough to do all these things at once. Furthermore, you don't really need to do all of them every single day. For one thing, throwing the garbage and checking expiration dates is something you can do more or less once a week, but there are also times in which things aren't necessary even if they haven't expired. In both cases, recurring and unforeseen, there is a chance you'll be doing something almost every day.

So you could probably distribute tasks on an every-other-day basis. But again, such a degree of freedom and routine is only attainable once you've moved past decluttering a major mess. Most cases of crisis are related to an attempt of everyday cleaning that is wrongfully performed on top of an underlying mess that hasn't really been addressed yet. That is why you need to take your time first and avoid getting impatient. If you succeed, your kitchen will work like a charm and allow the rest of the house to breathe.

A Common Pitfall: Cleaning Up After Visits

Because a good number of social activities are built around meals, there is a lot of room for the kitchen to get especially messy after visits. You can successfully master both major and everyday levels of mess on a day-to-day basis. However, when it comes to cooking up special dishes for a large number of people, you can still get trapped in square one all over again. Because of this, some people even prefer to hire a catering service and relieve themselves of all the work. Now, this is a feasible solution for extra special occasions, I'll admit that. But what happens when you just happen to get two, three small visits in a row? Maybe your friends came for dinner last night, then after two days your parents decided to drop by, and on the weekend one of your children received a visit from one of their friends. Before you know it, all these little minor events can get the kitchen, well —cluttered.

So it's clear we need to have an alternate strategy for things like this. Here we do exactly the same as in everyday kitchen tasks, but with the important concern of not letting things pile up. If you can afford to do so, do a couple power hour sessions the very night after your visitors left, or failing that, the following day. The usual set of utensils and cleaning products is the same. You just need to extend the efforts and bring things back to normal as quickly as possible. Keep in mind that this is by no means the only room in the house, so if you let the mess grow that's a guaranteed recipe for trouble. Take on this as if it were a major mess in the making and clean it up before it actually turns into one. If you really want to get back to normal, then there's no alternative but to do an emergency express clean-up, staying up a little late if necessary, but with the comfort of knowing you're doing the right thing.

Specific Tips and Tricks

- A wise use of the space under the sink

A sink usually comes embedded into a cabinet that is hollow underneath, which results in a big space being unused. Things are already designed to avoid this too; that's why there's usually doors under the sink. When we open those doors, the first things we usually find in sight are the plumbing and the drain trap. There will also surely be some other cable plugged into the wall for the dishwasher or the water heater, if you have one. My point is that it's a bit awkward down there, it's not ideal. But you still have a large piece of furniture there and enough room to store some things that might come in handy. To keep this place as neat as possible, it's a good idea to put shelving units there, specially measured for the size of your cabinet, if necessary. If you choose to go that way, make sure you get metal shelves because even in the best conditions there's some humidity there. Also, metal shelves are always much easier to clean. This solution will give more room to the place, which isn't that big in itself.

Having the trash can there is a classic solution, but the range of things you can do with that space is not that limited. In keeping with practicality, you can put replacement bags for when you throw out the trash and need to put a new bag on the can. The area is also ideal for jars and cleaning products you use to clean the rest of the kitchen. These are typically things you don't need to worry about getting a little humid, and the shelves will help keep them easily within your reach. By contrast, if you put cleaning tools in a bag and simply throw them down there, things can spill out of the bottles and get sticky. You won't even feel good about pulling that bag out of the sink, ever.

- A cooker extractor is vital

I'm sure you're familiar with them. They're these square things you find floating above the kitchen stove. They seemingly don't do that much, but they suck air from all your cooking and prevent other surfaces from getting covered in grease. This makes the job of dusting the kitchen much easier because the more it is covered with grease, the easier it is for dust to stick to utensils and surfaces. We hardly notice this day after day, but after a while it becomes painfully evident.

That's why you always need to get an extractor, and also open up your windows and ventilate the place on a daily basis.

And yes, extractors do need to be cleaned up every now and then. They're generally made of steel or aluminum, and the best way to clean them up is in the dishwasher. Aluminum filters tend to lose some shine after a few cleaning rounds, but they're cheaper. For me, that's just not that important. The main priority is cleanliness, but either way, it's something to keep in mind.

- Detergents and water: how to use and save them

Most modern dishwashers, whether in tablet or liquid soap, come with a degree of concentration that allows us to optimize to a certain degree. To avoid wasting detergent, we can try cutting the tablet in half or diluting the liquid soap in water. Mind you, this isn't advisable for day-to-day cleaning, at least not in my opinion. You can use it, though, for major cleaning sessions where you need to clean the floor and wall tiles thoroughly. These sessions usually come once a month, in my case. The thing is you must put detergent on tiles to remove the grease, so if you're not careful enough these sessions can be very costly in terms of detergent.

On the other end, while trying to be eco-friendly, you also need to track your water usage. Dishwashers are very good at this because they're designed to heat water and use it very efficiently. The human hand simply can't do that, no matter how hard we try, but if you don't have, or don't want to have a dishwasher, here's what you do. Lock the sink with the rubber cork and fill it to only one third of its capacity. Ideally, you'll have a sink with two sections, so you can use one for soap and one for rinsing. Use this method for around a dozen things, depending on how dirty they are, and repeat the procedure as many times as you need until all the dishes have been washed. This will allow you to keep things clean every day, while still not being wasteful with your water usage.

- How to avoid bad smells and give some color to the kitchen

The answer is easy: flowers. Now, you can go in two different ways on this. You can either get fresh flowers or dried flowers. In the first case, it is best if you can manage to have some way of getting the flowers from your own garden; we will actually cover this in a later chapter. It's important to do it this way because you can save a couple of bucks and also have a fancy pastime keeping some nice plants in your house. In the second case, again, you can dry flowers on your own or you can just get them at a store. The benefit of dry flowers is they last longer.

An important warning, though. Let us say your plumbing is rather old or it has malfunctions you haven't checked in a while. This will cause it to smell badly, but it would be a mistake to think that a bouquet of flowers will itself make much difference. First, real cleanliness has to be accomplished. That includes internal smells that are harder to remove. If you want flowers to really have an effect in your kitchen both as an ornament and as a freshener, then you must hire a plumber when things aren't going as they should in that area.

- The pantry: a tool or a liability?

This is probably more or less of a concern depending on the climate of the place you live in. Warm, humid cities are usually a place where you can't afford to leave food around for too long, even when it's still packaged. God forbid, you could find mice or even rats breaking boxes open and feeding off your leftovers. That's the last thing you need when you're quarrelling against the stress of a cluttered house, but it's important to address these possibilities, especially if you have a big family and groceries are equally big to match.

Basic groceries are the ones that save us from having to order takeout food every single time. In this sense, the pantry can be a veritable savior that allows you to avoid going to the market all too often. So try to get dry stuff, things that will resist the passage of time, like pasta, dried fruits, jars of pickles, or cans of tuna. Even if you don't use these things in every single recipe, they always come in handy when you run out of time and need to cook something quickly.

The downside, however, is the risk of not using everything you bought. To avoid this from happening, you need to have a weekly cooking schedule. That way you can cook according to pre-planned menus and have an idea of exactly what you'll be using and when. This helps save time and money while it also lets you eschew ugly surprises in the pantry. In other words, this room is no doubt a tool, but only if you can keep a good track of everything. And yes, you guessed it: that means yet more lists. At this point, it is actually worth mentioning that mobile apps are especially good at managing many lists at once. To avoid overwhelming yourself with handwritten lists, you should try them out until you find the one you prefer.

Key Takeaways

- Together with bathrooms, kitchens are the lungs of the house. The whole house will function properly if at the foundation these two places are okay.
- A kitchen is properly taken care of by doing two types of cleaning rounds, lighter ones every day and more thorough ones once a week.
- During daily rounds you're supposed to police the items you have in the fridge, the pantry, over the counters, and on the table.
- During weekly rounds, wash down the place from top to bottom using detergents, water, rags and other equipment.
- A basic trick of popular common sense: save up space by keeping the cleaning equipment under the sink.
- Using air fresheners only works if the place is clean, otherwise it mixes up with other smells and worsens things.
- Don't keep the pantry unattended. It is a very useful tool, but only as long as you keep good track of everything you store in it.

Chapter 5

The Bathroom(s)

"When a room becomes cluttered, the cause is usually more than physical"

— *Marie Kondo*

In keeping with our "lungs" metaphor, this is the second critical place of the whole house. Also, I'm using the bathroom(s) precaution here because unlike a kitchen, there can be any number of bathrooms in a single house, each as critical as the rest. And yes, the more you have, the more difficult it will be for you to take care of them all. Luckily, some are far more frequently used than others. A guest bathroom usually doesn't even have a shower and people only go there when you have guests, which doesn't happen every single day of the week. Then again, don't take that overly seriously because bathrooms are one of those places that can get really dirty if you give them a chance. If you don't want clutter to be a part of your daily life, then keeping bathrooms neat is simply a must.

Decluttering Advice

Cleaning bathrooms can be quite unfortunate for those who do it because they're one of the places people least notice when they get cleaned. Also, they are among the most noticeable when they haven't been cleaned. There seems to be no middle ground in between, which is kind of unfair. They are either totally forgotten or a total reason for embarrassment, even debate. People usually take it for granted that bathrooms must be clean and smell nice at all times, yet the duty of keeping them that way isn't very glamorous or even altogether appreciated.

We mustn't let that be a discouragement. Bathrooms must be under constant supervision throughout the week and also, once a week, we need to clean them up thoroughly. That's the ideal combination, and everyone in the house must be involved in it so that it is always a shared load. Of course, you want to include your kids in this so they can learn how to do it as they grow up. If and when you do, just make sure you keep them away from the toilet. Give them other tasks so they can see you at work but also keep away from the toughest zones. Always use rubber gloves, even a mask to cover your nose and mouth, and show your kids that certain areas are to be treated with special care because they can be very dirty and potentially infectious.

On the flipside, bathrooms are usually a small space, rarely bigger than a 4x4 meter room. That makes them a task you can undertake in a few minutes each day, and only spend more time in when it's time to do the weekly tidy up. As a general rule, you should never put too much stuff in any bathroom, be it your main one or those for guests. Because they are small rooms, they can get cluttered rather quickly. Maintaining order in them is essential to a good organization of space. The gist of it is you should get floating furniture wherever possible, so as to free up valuable floor space. Keep things practical and easy to clean. Cleaning bathrooms does not need to be a chore. Those who keep theirs artfully arranged know how much that is true.

Main Bathrooms

Here's the thing: these are the ones where you need to spend the most time on the design stage. We will not always have the privilege of starting with a blank sheet of paper, though. This often happens only when we get the chance to build a house from scratch, and even then it's not guaranteed. You could be buying a house designed by someone else; in that case you're stuck with whatever kind of layout they decided to use for the bathroom. Either way, what I actually mean by spending time on the design stage is you should make the most out of whatever bathroom you have.

That means not rushing to the daily and weekly cleaning sessions just yet. Before that, you need to declutter that room and turn it into a veritable masterpiece of practicality. If you can do that, every cleaning session will feel like a breeze. Even more, when you do clean, you won't be able to help but rejoice at how well you fixed that place up.

So let's make a list of the basics. In every bathroom we can find a basin cabinet, a sink, a toilet, a shower, and some bars for hanging towels and other utensils. Those are more or less the items that make a bathroom, but they're also things that are fixed in place. The real problem comes with all the stuff we put on top of that. In the case of those for guests, the main difference is we probably have no shower and sometimes no basin cabinet, but we need not concern ourselves with guest bathrooms for now.

Decluttering Advice

First off, find out how many things you have in that bathroom. If it helps, you can put them on a sofa or over your bed so as to get an idea of the volume they occupy. Let's see. What do you have there?

- Toothbrushes and toothpaste
- A shaver/razor
- Deodorant
- Soap
- Face and body cream
- Makeup
- Medicine/pills
- Shampoo
- Toilet paper (and a toilet paper bag to keep replacements going)
- Cotton swabs
- Nail clippers
- Hand and body towels

The list could go on. In any case, if you put all that together, you could easily fill up a small case, perhaps even more. So where are you going to put it all?

- Electrical gadgets

For one thing, similar to the kitchen, you probably have an empty space underneath the sink. Keep in mind the plumbing is there, so you can't store things that could get ruined with humidity. Therefore if you have an electric razor, an electric epilator, or any other gadgets you plug in or use with batteries, of course, don't ever put them there, no matter how convenient it may seem. These gadgets usually have cables that are difficult to fold and put away, so it can be very tempting to put them under the sink. Well, if you trust your plumbing to never have any problems, go ahead. However, my advice is to avoid these risks instead of pushing your luck.

- Toilet paper

A big concern I grappled with for quite some time is the sheer size of the toilet paper bag. Because it's wrapped in plastic and humidity can't get to the paper inside, I have tried many times to fit it under the sink, with no success. Then it finally hit me: this bag itself looks ugly. The reason I want to hide it is because I don't like it. But it wasn't until I managed to think outside the box that I came up with the perfect solution. You know what I did? I took all the rolls out of the box and installed a wooden bar vertically to the side of the toilet itself. The bar has hooks on both extremes so you can undo them and put new rolls on one side while taking them off the other. If well executed, this neat little trick is also a nice ornament that contrasts marvelously with the cold surface of the tiles on the wall.

You also need to keep track of how these ideas work in real life. For example, after I implemented this toilet paper dispenser, I realized the moisture from taking showers was causing the rolls of paper to wrinkle a little. One day my daughter came to me and said she couldn't rip off the paper because it was a little sticky. In the end we had to install a glass bathing box, which took even longer to finish, but now I'm happy to say toilet paper is always within reach and it doesn't get wet.

- The trash can

Decluttering Advice

Because of the delicate nature of your disposals, this is one of the things you must watch closely during your daily cleaning. But, even before thinking about that, there's one key decision I think we need to discuss: whether your trash-can will be an open basket or whether it will have a lid. On the one hand, you don't want to look at your disposals, which can make a lid rather tempting. On the other hand, especially if you have small children, that lid is likely to get dirty real quick. You want to keep those two things in mind and balance them out before making a decision.

This is how I solved the issue. At first, I decided I would go with a plastic can while my children were still learning to use the toilet. That made cleaning easier to spot and to clean. Then as time went by, I got a cane basket with a separate cover and I kept it open during times in which I knew my kids were awake—at least until they grew up a little more. That way, throwing paper was still easy to them, but closing the can whenever necessary was still possible.

- Piped heating

This is one of my favorites. You see, my husband's parents are German, and over in Europe people love to install piped heating in their houses. They just can't live without it, and I admit I got hooked after a winter I spent at my in-laws' cabin. I was showering one day and as soon as I turned off the water I felt a little chilly. Nothing too serious, but it was snowing outside, so the climate was cold in general. Then I reached out for a towel, I picked it up from what looked like any generic metal bar attached to the wall. But it wasn't. The towel felt warm and perfect as it came in contact with my skin. I was amazed and befuddled, so as soon as I got out I asked: what's that thing you have in the bathroom to hang your towels?

Put simply, it's a piece of esthetic plumbing that comes out of your wall and looks a little like a small metal ladder. In it you have about two to three levels in which you can hang different sizes of towels, and as they hang there, they get both dry and warm, ready for you to use at all times. It's something that takes time to install and it isn't exactly cheap, but it runs on natural gas, so once it's there it *is* pretty affordable. I can tell you my kids love it, and as for me, whenever I finish one of those deep cleaning sessions I do once a month, there is nothing like taking a shower and pulling out a warm towel.

- Shelves and cabinets

Whenever possible, try to install floating ones. That way you don't lose floor space on extra furniture, which is especially important when a bathroom isn't huge. For the perfect arrangement, you need to look back at that list of hygiene effects, measure a thing or two if necessary, and then hire a qualified carpenter to do the job for you. My advice: stick to metal shelves to avoid any future problems with moisture. As you may remember, I said the same thing in the kitchen section—precisely about the area underneath the sink too. In both cases, the choice of material must be pragmatic rather than aesthetic.

I know you might be thinking wood would be a nice option too. Provided you have it laminated or heavily varnished, I reckon it could work, but I've seen these solutions fail after only a few months where sinks are too humid. Keep in mind wood is basically a natural sponge, so the way it reacts to moisture is different from that of metal. Wood can bend, shrink, and expand, thus altering the whole shape of the shelves. By contrast, metal *can* rust with moisture, but put a layer of waterproofing paint on it and it will stay the same for ages.

This is important because the space underneath the sink, like in the kitchen, is a key place to put stuff that would otherwise clutter the bathroom. That being said, you should never store other items besides replacement soaps, shampoo bottles, and toothpaste tubes. The things you use every day should always go on open shelves that are within easy reach when you stand in front of the sink. It's important you try to avoid getting extra pieces of furniture because the amount of space is very limited. If you find shelves don't suffice, take that as a sign to reduce bathroom items instead of cluttering the place even more with furniture.

* * *

Some of the solutions I suggested, of course, require more work on the backend. You need to take measures of the space and hire technicians to do the things you planned, so yes, it takes a while. But it's also worth it. Once again, that is precisely what I meant by "spending time on the design stage." Once you know the kind of bathroom you have and the things you need to fit in there, some things are going to be easy to solve and some will require you to think harder and put a little extra work in them. There is no way one single kind of solution will work for everything because the sheer variety of things we use in a bathroom is very large.

Also, even if you don't like some of the solutions I used, what matters is you adopt the philosophy behind them. When it comes to your main bathroom, you can spare no effort. Do the hard work and install shelves in exactly the corners you find most helpful, practical, and good looking. This place has to feel more cozy, and that means you pick materials with both practicality and appearance in mind. Getting a personal bathroom to work and look exactly as you want can take weeks, but once you have them exactly the way you want, daily and weekly cleaning rounds are much easier, even pleasant.

Guest Bathrooms

For this, we must take a U-turn. If the spirit of organizing a personal bathroom is about arranging many things in an elegant way, in the case of guest bathrooms elegance has to be achieved in quite the opposite way. You want to keep as little stuff as you possibly can in there. That makes them look neat before the eyes of those who will use them, and it also helps make cleaning a much simpler task.

A guest usually doesn't need much more than soap, toilet paper, a hand towel, and a trash can. I would recommend you use liquid soap and that you get a dark color for the towel because it helps make stains unnoticeable. It's not that you will leave that towel there forever. In fact, you should replace it after each visit. The thing is, though, that white towels get dirty real quick and you don't want your guests asking whether you can give them a new towel for their hands.

By way of decoration and a way to give the place a nice smell, I usually like to go with cane baskets because their natural color always contrasts nicely with the floor and wall tiles. I myself put one over the toilet tank and one to the side of the sink and then I pour dried flowers on them to spread the smell. On the other hand, we shouldn't forget our goal is to both find good looking solutions and declutter the house in general. That means if you haven't got a pair of cane baskets, you mustn't go buying them and adding more stuff to your home. Take a look around the house and think of alternatives. Some neat ideas would be to recycle old glass jelly or pickle jars. These will look nice on their own. You just wash them real well, get rid of the lid, and you're done. Dried flowers look very nice on glass because of their color.

As for the trash can, it would seem at first the ideal scenario is that you have a metallic one with an opening pedal at the bottom. That's both sturdy and elegant, although the pedal mechanism can sometimes stop working. Instead of going that way, just keep in line with the main spirit of your endeavor and use whatever you already have. Avoid buying new things at all costs. Whatever trash can you have serves the purpose; you just need to make sure you visit it every day on your daily cleaning rounds. I personally prefer not to put a plastic bag there because if I did, that would be harmful to the environment. I use the cleaning rounds to move whatever waste I find there into the main trash can.

Daily and Weekly Routines

- Daily round

Daily maintenance should not take us more than a few minutes. During these rounds, you're not so much cleaning up as you're keeping an eye on things. You're supposed to use these rounds to check whether those trash cans aren't full yet, whether you need to replace the soap, whether towels are ready to be sent for a wash, etc. You also need to take a look at faucets, sinks, and toilets in search of any unexpected dirtiness that can't wait until the weekly round. If there is, those few minutes might turn into a half-hour duty, but that shouldn't happen too often. Why? Primarily because, at least with your main bathroom, everyone in the house must learn to use it conscientiously, avoiding cleaning work for later and trying to make habits themselves the first form of "cleaning."

At any rate, the worst thing that could happen is that you find a toilet is dirty. When that happens, you just keep things simple. Put a pair of gloves, squirt a little bleach in there and give it a quick brush, then grab a sponge and also give it a quick wipe on the outside too. That shouldn't take more than 15 to 20 minutes. You can also give both bathrooms a sweep, which is always easy because of the tiled floors, and that's it. Other things are certainly going to pop up as you go through this routine, but just add them to your to-do list. Apart from extenuating circumstances, it's important that these daily rounds don't turn into a "thing."

- Weekly round

This round will take you about an hour, so you can do it on weekends, preferably during daylight so as to locate dirty areas better. The theme of this round is cleaning surfaces before you move on to the things you would normally check on a daily round. You must give a thorough cleaning to everything that's made of ceramic: sinks, bidets (if you have them), toilets, shower floors, or bathtubs. To avoid scratching surfaces, use a loofah. In fact, I would recommend you have the entire kit ready to use inside a bucket at all times: give or take – a loofah, detergent, bleach, a sponge, and a cloth. It's important you use different sponges and loofahs for all areas because you don't want to put a sponge in the sink that was being used to clean the floor only five minutes earlier.

If you were to find a drain clogged, which is one of the toughest things to solve, you need to unscrew it and pull what you can through the hole. What you find is generally going to be hair and soap debris. Because of this, you can also think about putting a metal sump on top of the drain to catch the hair before it gets in there. Unclogging a dirty drain is probably the most unpleasant part about cleaning bathrooms, but it's the number one reason they start smelling bad, so we can't afford to ignore it. Keep an eye on all drains every week to avoid major problems of this nature coming up. Now, if you find this problem does get out of control and is too hard to solve, put a spoonful of caustic soda right in the drain and wait half an hour, then pour water in there to rinse and drag all the dirt. After you're done, make sure you also recommend everybody in the house to avoid washing hair down the drain.

When the hardest part is over, you can move on to the things you would do on a regular day. Scrubbing surfaces and unclogging drains are the two central tasks of a weekly round. Besides that, you basically repeat what you would normally do on weekdays.

Key Takeaways

- There are two types of bathrooms in all houses, one for the family and one (or more) for visitors. In each case the requirements are fairly different.
- In the main bathroom you should take advantage of walls and the space under the sink to locate shelves

and store your stuff on them. This is important to free up space on the floor and improve circulation.
- In guest bathrooms you need to store even less things and keep ornaments to a minimum. If possible, use ornamental pieces as fresheners as well.
- Like the kitchen, bathrooms too require you to perform weekly and daily cleaning rounds.
- Keep daily rounds as short as possible, limiting yourself to renew things that may have been used up, sweeping, and not much else.
- On weekly rounds, put aside a couple of hours and do a thorough cleaning up with water, disinfectant, and detergent.

Chapter 6

Bedrooms

"When life gets hectic, self-care practically flies out of the window—but if you want to successfully maintain everything then it is going to become your best friend"

— *Lynsey Crombie*

Bedrooms have a lot of layers and they come in different forms depending on who uses them. However, one common concern to all bedrooms alike is that because they house a lot of cloth items, they need to be constantly dusted. Bedrooms are dust magnets and they are also places where people tend to spend a significant amount of time, whether resting, killing time, or playing around. Therefore they should always be kept ventilated and free of dust to avoid respiratory allergies.

Dust isn't all I want to cover in this chapter, but it's an essential part, so it's worth discussing at some length here. According to an article in *The Washington Post* (Filipelli, 2019), what we usually call dust is a mishmash of detritus from pets, dead human skin cells, decomposed insects, fibers from the carpet, bedding clothes, and more. Dust really is a composite of everything that moves around there in the world, splits over time into minuscule particles and then floats around through wind and atmospheric pressure, slowly lurking into our lungs and having an overall negative effect on our health. In fact, a lot of the fatigue we experience when the house is a mess comes from this. We don't notice it so much precisely because it's sort of invisible, but it's there.

This is a major reason for concern because all bedrooms should be the place in the house where people can rest at ease. Apart from the office, it is probably the place where we spend most consecutive hours in our life. Depending on the quality of our sleep, we can wake up in all sorts of moods. Whether or not we were able to rest properly determines the attitude and energy we will have throughout the day. Even for other cleaning tasks, a tired, poorly rested person is often likely to perform worse than in normal conditions. To avoid this, we need to make sure bedrooms are organized, comfortable, and dust free.

The Room and the Age of its Occupant

If you have kids, their rooms need to be thought of in quite a different way. You still need to think about dust and ventilation, but above all you need to give them space to move around and not worry about getting things dirty. This, for instance, has led me to not put carpeting in my children's rooms until they grew up a little. It also led me to leave walls alone and let them get dirty without worrying too much about it. Kids often find it very fun to leave their prints on the wall, and we shouldn't give cleanliness precedence over their recreational activities. The bottom line is you can't impose an urge for cleanliness on kids. You just have to let them be and make them learn slowly and by example.

As I said before, the more you incorporate kids into the cleaning sessions you do around the house, the quicker they will become concerned about cleanliness themselves. They will grow appreciative of their own space and start actively thinking about how they want to arrange it. To you as parents, the most important thing is you encourage that feeling by giving them freedom to choose and compare the first solutions they implement on their own. You can't impose an urge on them, but if you show them there are healthy ways of addressing clutter in the home, and having fun while doing it, they will learn that and become your main assistants in the job.

The Bed

A common practice in the old days, and still to this day in certain traditional places, was to keep the bed in quite a more cumbersome way than we do now. Linens, fancy pillowcases, and several layers of blankets were a normal thing in people's lives. Now, I don't know what your specific habits are in this regard, but I personally don't have so much stuff on the bed. Even then, I learned the hard way that every ornament on the bed is an extra thing to worry about. Take for instance those big beds we see in housekeeping magazines. They look as though they were covered at least halfway by an army of pillows. Where do you think those have to go when you actually get into bed? Well, if you don't want to just throw them over the carpet, you need to get a special storage area for them. Then all of a sudden you're making room for pillows, when your main objective was to get rid of unnecessary hassles and keep things simple.

That kind of image is more intended to lure you into buying new bed clothes than anything else and you can certainly find better solutions. But once again, my advice to you is to avoid buying more new stuff and look at what you have right there. Then on the basis of that, think about what you don't really need. In my case, this process meant pulling out some extra blankets and a couple ornamental pillows nobody was using. Now every bed in the house is stripped to the absolute basics: a mattress, a single sheet covering it, a comforter on top, and a single pillow for each person. Only what is necessary—no more, no less.

You might be wondering about what happens during cold winters, and with good reason. My answer is simple. Let the heating do its job and forget about it. No one really relies solely on their bed covers to keep themselves warm at night, so it'd be silly to turn to that as the number one priority. Instead, make sure your heating works well and strip your beds as much as possible. Put every excess item you pull out of them together and give them away as a donation. A couple extra benefits from this is that the beds won't collect so much dust anymore, helping to clean up the air you breathe in your room. Moreover, you will spend less than five minutes a day making the bed. Who doesn't like that?

The Bedside Tables

This is perhaps more of a personal thing. Everyone has their own way of making use of a bedside table, and by all means everyone should, but the point we're trying to get at here is preventing excessive, unnecessary accumulation. And how do you do that? I think the best way is to avoid getting big, complicated bedside tables with drawers, lockers and whatnot. If you really want to declutter the bedroom, you need to be serious about this and get tables consisting of nothing more than two shelves held together by wooden pillars. I normally wouldn't tell you to buy more stuff, but if you don't happen to have one of these, I'd advise you to go get one. They really help keep things to a minimum.

Hollow bedside tables are the answer to every person who has gotten them stuffed with pills, phone chargers, money, documents, bills, and all sorts of other things that one tends to put in the drawer and forget about. If you think about it, none of what you put in there is ever getting much use thereafter, so why put it there in the first place? It takes up room, it looks awful when you actually open the drawers, and it even causes you to lose important stuff you really need. Don't be that kind of person. Get hollow bedside tables instead. I'll bet you 90% of the clutter we tend to build up in those places comes from the simple fact that they're available. The moment they disappear, untidiness starts fading almost on its own.

One common mistake with bedside tables is we often try to arrange them as if they were sample pieces. We do this because that's how they look on dedicated websites and magazines about the subject. And no, my intention is not to belittle the merit of interior design. I am simply trying to highlight the fact that you need not opt for things only on the basis that they look nice in a photograph.

For example, I wouldn't ever recommend you put dried flowers or any other kind of freshener on your bedside table. The smell would be far too close to you while you sleep and you might develop a headache or maybe even an allergy. All you should have on this table is an alarm clock, a lamp, the book you're currently reading, and perhaps a medicine dispenser if you need to have one within reach. Other than that, try to keep this area clean, and keep other necessities in your medicine cabinet or on your dressing table. Keep the bedside area clean because that's where you're supposed to rest. Having it too busy will make that harder to do.

The Dressing Table

Chances are you don't necessarily have one of these, but if you do, it's an area to keep very much under control. Think of it as a kind of extension of your bathroom. You let it loose too much and the whole bedroom will look like you're managing a makeup workshop. We all know how hard it is to keep creams and makeup in order. Normally, they are put on shelves and drawers of all different sizes. That is all fine, but the real problem doesn't start there. The thing is all these self-care utensils, creams, balms, and lotions are used on a daily basis, usually at times of great haste to leave for the office or some other similar commitment. There is really no other way of doing it since we usually "get ready to go out" precisely when we're about to go out, not several hours in advance. Thus we throw a lot of these items around in utter disregard for whether they'll land in the right place, whether they'll break into smaller pieces and spread over the floor. We can't always help but do these things and the price we pay is that the dressing table looks rather unwelcoming most of the time.

If you have makeup enthusiasts at home or you yourself are one, then you must probably relate to such situations. Then again, makeup enthusiasts are generally experts at keeping their equipment nice and tidy. Either way, when cleaning up

Decluttering Advice

this area of the room, don't just settle with dusting off everything in sight. Empty the furniture where you keep your makeup and study what you have. This is similar to what we discussed about the bathroom. Think about what you use regularly, what you only use on special occasions, and lastly, what you barely ever use. Most people tend to find there are a bunch of things they haven't used in a long time or that have already expired. If this happens to you too, that means you should throw it away. We all hesitate to do this by asking: What if I need it at some point? But let's be honest. That just never happens.

Once you're done reviewing and classifying, organize it all by categories, assigning each item a specific place within the whole array, so that you know where to find it later and have easy access to it. You could probably feel the need to purchase an organizer for this. In regular circumstances, that would probably be a good idea, but remember you're not just organizing your makeup here. If you really want an organizer, go around the house and look for the next best thing among whatever stuff you already have.

I for one have found an average house disposes of a lot of tupperware on a regular basis. Bottles, lunchboxes, and some more elaborate things too. At first this mortified me because of what it meant to the environment, but now I've implemented another command-z technique on our tupperware. That way if I find that I need some sort of receptacle, I just go and check our tupperware box and see whether something fits my needs, and very often I do. Likewise, for this and every other challenge in the house, always try to be resourceful and use the things that you already have at hand.

The Closet

In a way, closets are similar to pantries in that they can feel extra helpful when they're big. In that sense, those of you who have a walk-in closet must feel utterly lucky. But the more space you have, the harder it is to keep it all under control, and this is only worsened by the fact that people often put on clothes with the same haste as when they put on makeup. That is, in a rush and throwing things around. Daily activities force us to run from one place to another without paying much attention.

Big, spacious closets with lots of space, drawers, and shelves are wonderful. No one denies that. The question is how you can use all those resources in a way that feels both ample and easy to manage. The way I see it, the answer lies in devising a plan of use and accommodation that adjusts to the days of the week. Seven days, seven changes of clothes.

Start by going through your week as you normally would and take note of the things that you wore during that time. Then stop tracking yourself for one or two weeks and get back to taking notes for another full week. Tell everyone in the house to do the same. The result should give you all a broad idea of the things that you wear, and the reason you will skip a couple weeks is to avoid feeling self-conscious about the fact that you're tracking what you wear.

No one really uses the exact same set of clothes every time, but it would surprise you to see how much repetition there is. This realization should accomplish two things: it should help you see how little you need to shop for new clothes, and it should also give you an idea of what you need to have at hand the most. That way you can prioritize all the space in your

Decluttering Advice

closet according to that criteria and thus avoid moving things around unnecessarily. More often than not, the reason we move too much stuff around and throw our clothes around is because we're looking for something that wasn't properly placed from the beginning.

The same goes for your children. You should explain to them that certain things such as underwear, t-shirts, the jacket they wear the most, etc. are to be kept within easy reach. As with their bathroom, if they have their own, they should be free to decide how they arrange their closet, but with you as their guidance. Tell them why it's important to put things they regularly use as close as possible, and also remind them to avoid putting clothes in the closet when they're already dirty.

Over time you'll also identify things you almost never use but don't want to throw away. These are items like rain coats, winter jackets, sleeping bags and the like. To store these items in the most effective way and in the smallest possible space, vacuum bags are a great solution. If you haven't heard of them, they are like regular plastic bags, but with an airtight seal from which you can literally vacuum all the air inside after you've closed the bag. That effectively compresses whatever you put inside so as to limit the space they occupy. You can put that stuff on the top cabinets of the closet and thus free up a lot of space, which is very helpful, provided you don't put anything there you might end up needing the next day. All in all, that's the main principle: Any organizational solution requires you know what you wear the most and what you wear the least.

Certain things, however, might never come out to see the light of day again. After you put them away in some dark corner of your closet, either in plastic vacuum bags or in suitcases, you may forget they even exist. But they do, and they take up space. A question then lurks to the surface, but of course we neglect it as long as we can. No one looks forward to the day of throwing away a bunch of old suits they've never worn in the past ten years. For some reason the very thought of it is slightly gloomy. Either way, you should throw all that stuff away. Moreover, because we're mostly talking about clothes here, these are all things you can donate to someone who will put them to much better use than you.

If you really can't help but feel unconvinced, you can send some of this stuff to the basement and put it in cardboard boxes. Mind you, they won't stop taking up valuable space that way; they'll just be a little easier to forget. But anyway, you can put them there as a kind of pre-donation or pre-trash area. Don't forget to label the boxes and add a reminder on your calendar, once every month if possible, to remind you every month that has gone by without you making use of this stuff. This routinary reminder, as it did with me, will help convince you that some things simply need to be thrown away and that avoiding the same problem in the future means buying less clothes as well.

Key Takeaways

- Bedrooms are dust gatherers, especially when disorganized. The basic goal of keeping them neat and clean is improving the quality of life you have in them.
- We sometimes imagine something that looks nice but isn't very functional. You mustn't have more furniture than you can handle, and what you do have must be regularly decluttered.

Decluttering Advice

- Set a place for every hygiene product, garment, or electric accessory. When you do, prioritize the things you use more regularly and put things you rarely use at the bottom.
- Same with clothes. Track what you wear the most and what you wear only occasionally. A well-organized closet should reflect that same distinction and facilitate access to things that are regularly taken in and out of it.
- Clothes you don't use should be donated or thrown away, but if you feel bad doing so, put them in cardboard boxes in the basement.
- Set a monthly reminder to check those boxes so as to gradually convince you to let them go.
- A good organizational operation is one that sustains itself for how well it fits your habits and schedules. Avoiding clutter starts by getting to the point where you have that kind of organization.

Chapter 7
Common Areas

"Your home is your oasis. It's meant to be an escape from the work and stress of the outside world, not a chaotic place where you simply store your stuff"

— *Cassandra Aarssen*

These aren't as fundamental or as difficult to maintain as the lungs of the house, which is not to say they're not at all important. Primarily, they are the ones that offer the first real image of ourselves and our way of life to everyone who comes into the house. Even for you and your family, they are the first thing you see when you walk through the door, and depending on the day that you had, they truly have the power to set our mood in very specific ways. Coming home tired and eager to unplug for a little while gives these areas a special importance in day-to-day life, so we must try to keep them up to both tasks:

- Presenting ourselves to visitors.

- Giving us a warm and welcoming reception when coming in from the outside.

Both these tasks are in direct connection to the need of decluttering a home. The will to give visitors a nice impression is always a reason we crack our heads and worry too much. Similarly, when the house is a mess and we get used to arriving there day after day, we don't notice it at once, but the effect this has on us is very detrimental. It's a little bit like having the bedroom filled with dust and developing a respiratory syndrome as a consequence: it feels awful, but the main thing is that it could have been avoided.

The worst thing that can happen as a result of this problem is that you gradually stop inviting people to come visit. It isn't that you stopped enjoying social life; it's just that you're embarrassed and wish to live this mess in private. But let me tell you right now that is the worst mistake you could make. No matter how embarrassing it may feel, having people come to your house is an incentive to keep bringing the house back to normal, and afterwards, to keep it clean thereafter. You should instead consider visits as a nice pretext to bring the subject to the table and get useful tips from both friends and family. The reality is everyone faces pretty much the same problem in their own house, one way or another. If you open up, you'll be surprised at the sheer number of interesting, useful tips people can give you.

Now, we need not worry so much about common areas, as I said. For all their notoriety, when people feel self-conscious about the state of their foyer, for instance, that is generally the sign of something much deeper. It isn't that their foyer alone needs serious decluttering; rather, it is the most visible manifestation of the state their entire house is in. Do you share this opinion? I think this way because, in my view, we all tend to hide untidiness from the view of others. Thus when this untidiness has finally made its way into the common areas, that is usually a sign that we can no longer hide what lies behind. So, let's go through each of these common areas and see what can be done about them.

The Foyer

In order to look at common areas with a renovated view, it is necessary to break the strength of habits. We need to go back to that same place we go through every day, but outside the context in which we regularly do. At first, I was able to do this by pausing after I'd entered the foyer and looking back. I was either very tired and eager to go take a nap or loaded with a lot of unfinished work. Either way, I halted my progression and walked back.

I started taking note of all the little shortcomings that the entrance to the house caused me and the rest of the family. It mostly had to do with things all of us would leave there while still distracted, coming in from the outside world. We would leave keys, umbrellas, shoes and snow boots, coats, bags, and a whole bunch of other things. These were things that we all intended to leave there, but the mere way in which we did, sort of relieving ourselves from the burden of the day's occupations, that's what caused all the mess. We didn't quite put things in their place. In fact, it couldn't be said that these things actually had a place to begin with. We would just toss things here and there, making the entrance a very displeasing place.

Decluttering Advice

- What the foyer needs to do for us

The bare minimum is to have a space to leave our street clothes and shoes, those that we leave when we enter the house but that we will need later to go back outside. Beside this, it would also be nice to have a place for an umbrella, a coat, a purse, or a backpack. So, one thing is pretty clear: The foyer needs to have a lot of storage room. Nothing particularly fancy, just practical furniture and, in fact, made in a way that we won't mind if it gets dirty over time. That means wooden furniture, preferably unpainted so that it won't show stains all too easily or, at least, we won't mind if it does.

- Small things and accessories

You should also consider that, in passing, you'll be leaving a bunch of small things in the foyer. There's no use in giving them a proper place, though, because you're likely to pick them up again within a few minutes or hours. What to do, then? I think the best solution is to have one of the furniture pieces act as both a reservoir for shoes down below, but with the height of a table so you can use the top on which to place stuff. Moreover, I would advise you to avoid getting any drawers on this piece because if things aren't fully in sight, you're likely to forget them. In other words, apart from the shoe racks, nothing in the foyer should turn into a serious storage unit.

To have some level of organization on this table of sorts, you can incorporate open, colorful containers. For example, I use a handmade bowl for the keys. It looks so nice, all my visitors comment on it. Plus no one forgets to leave their keys there, so we haven't had to make emergency copies in a long time.

- What if you don't have a foyer?

Not all houses are equipped with a dedicated room for this purpose. In case your house doesn't either, don't worry. Most of the tasks a foyer fulfills can fit perfectly in an ordinary entrance corridor. Leaving your coat, taking your shoes off – these are all things you do in passing anyway. Just arrange everything to the sides and be sure to leave plenty of clear space in the center.

The Dining Room

In some cases, this section and the next are likely to be arranged within one single area of the house. If that's your case, the principles are the same; you just need to start from the idea that you have less space than regular. But that's not so much a disadvantage as it is an opportunity. In fact, having the dining and living room merged into a single area can be used to implement quite interesting layouts. For instance, you can put a credenza behind the sofa to mark a sort of half wall between the two areas and put ornaments and some hanging plants on top. This gives the living-room a charisma of its own and helps make small spaces look less cramped.

At any rate, regardless of the size and kind of dining room you're interested in decluttering, you must think thoroughly about the shape and size of this room. You need to make a list of all the furniture and decorative elements to place them in a way that takes advantage of the space. Having everything well placed is the best way to make a room appear less small than it actually is. It also helps with circulation, which is fundamental both for visitors as well as for cleaning. I would say a good 70% of the dining room arrangement comes down to having good circulation. The remaining 30% is about showcasing some of your nicest items, making the place look not just intelligently organized, but also interesting and pretty. I know you're in this primarily to improve the order of the house, but when it comes to common areas, a lot of it has to do with how you present them to outsiders—so make sure everything fits within a coherent decor style for the room.

To be clear, by this I do not mean you should buy more stuff to fit the collection you saw in an interior design magazine. There's nothing wrong with following professional advice and shopping around for new stuff, but that's not the point here. What I mean is you must take a deep look at what you have and come up with solutions based on that. All decluttering targets are going to be met if you impose on yourself the restriction of having to use what is already there in front of you.

In my case, for example, that meant figuring out how to display my favorite tableware even though I didn't have a display case with glass doors for people to see. Spoiler alert: my kitchen is open to the dining room and it has open wooden shelves above the counter, so I put my tableware over there. It's not the first solution I had in mind, which was to buy a display cabinet, but that would have taken up valuable space around the dining table.

Another example is I used to have a white crochet tablecloth that would always get way too dirty after dinner parties. Spotting the stains would make me very nervous and after a while I realized, because my dining table is made of glass, that I didn't really need the tablecloth. I washed it thoroughly one last time, cut it into smaller pieces and started using it as a cover for the sofa and the armchairs in the living room. In other words, I made cleaning the dining table a much easier task overnight, while also coming up with a nice decorative piece.

- Removing unused clutter and being smart with space

One of the most common things you find on dining room tables are papers. I mean everything from long forgotten documents to magazines, books, receipts, and even correspondence. Until you take the time to sort through them and classify them in groups, this is just excess stuff that badly needs your attention. They make the place look cluttered and not too elegant, so what should you do about them? Are they all things you can throw away or not?

First off, don't wait for the perfect time to sort through these papers. Pick them all up at once and put them on the dining table, then sort them out into groups according to where they ought to go afterwards. You might not finish in one single session, but the sheer fact of having started will give you courage to finish it off not too late in the future. And don't fall for the typical approach we sometimes take: "oh, I think I might need this at some point, maybe I shouldn't throw it away." Whenever we say that, I guarantee you almost 99% of the time we're just looking for an excuse.

To keep the dining room from looking stuffed and uncomfortable, make sure you police the amount of paper waste that ends up being left there. It takes only a few days for things to pile back up again, so you need to be both vigilant and persistent about it.

- Tablecloths, curtains, carpeting, and other potential liabilities

When it comes to areas where people are supposed to eat, it is especially important to avoid using fabrics and materials that can catch dirt too easily. As a general rule, it's a bad idea to have a carpet underneath the table. This might not be your case, but if it is, just take it out of there, wash it, and put it somewhere else. Along the same lines, I would say it's also better to get rid of tablecloths. I know we use them because they look nice, plus we sometimes get them as gifts and don't have a choice but to use them.

However, in my view they're among the main reasons a dining room can start looking rather dirty. Think of them as spider webs that are designed to trap little pieces of spilled food, crumbs, stains and so on. By leaving a tablecloth there, you're basically doing two things that will undoubtedly make any home clutter crisis you're facing much worse: You're opening the door for dirt to come into your eating times, and you're giving yourself an extra cleaning task when you could easily have avoided it.

Things like curtains, when they're especially bulky, and all other types of ornamental fabrics in the dining room have to be rethought from the same angle. We might feel a bit hesitant by thinking the place won't look as nice if we take them down. But think about it in these terms: If the goal is to declutter a home, then there's no way looks can take precedence over practicality, cleanliness, and order. If you give that mindset the centerpiece it rightfully deserves, you will see how nothing looks as attractive as a place that looks functional and effortlessly well kept.

The Living Room

Together with the dining room, this is a place that is 100% intended for social activities. Now, I know I said we should avoid the excessive use of cloth decorations in the dining room, but that is not as critical in the living room because its primary function isn't eating. That being said, the coffee table is often used for pastries and hot beverages on a regular basis. This is a potential source of trouble because unlike the dining room, the living room is usually carpeted. In fact, most living rooms often feature a thick, plush carpet that is basically a magnet for spillovers.

For this reason, a big portion of our cleaning rounds for common areas will have to be reserved for the living room. This is a place we can't strip down to the bare minimum. We actually want it to look attractive, so in this case decluttering must go hand in hand with a little bit of looks.

A good option for having a nice looking, yet still uncluttered living room is multifunctional furniture. For example, there are armchairs with trunks under the cushions or tables with built-in drawers. Every furniture with tools of this kind will help you store things without too much effort and without them being noticeable at all. They really can help bring back the living room to having a clean look.

If you don't have furniture of this kind, there is still an alternative. Let's say, for example, that you have a coffee table that is hollow underneath. You can still find smaller drawered units, similar to bedside tables but smaller, that will fit perfectly in that space. You can also adapt floating shelves in areas where people don't circulate much. Just with these two

Decluttering Advice

solutions, I guarantee you will find enough room to put some stuff that would look ugly if left out in the open.

At the same time, this extra space is not to be abused. The surest way to avoid this is getting rid of things you don't use. A living room can gather just as much paper waste as the dining room, perhaps even more. When it comes to keeping this place tidy, you must be aware of how much space you have to store stuff. Keep track of accumulating objects to make sure they don't ever exceed that storing room because that's when clutter starts looking back at you.

- What's an ornament and what is just clutter

Because they are meant mostly for visits, the dining room and the living room are in particular danger of being filled with ornaments. Moreover, some of these ornaments are going to be gifts you received from your parents, your in-laws, or just some friends. These people are going to want to see their gift on display whenever they visit, but after a few gifts have come in, are there any extra shelves for you to continue putting all of them on display? How can you get out of that vicious circle and start removing unnecessary ornaments that only take up space?

Start by remembering what we discussed in Chapter Three. You don't need to keep people's gifts out of guilt. Just be honest with them and tell them about your major decluttering quest. They have houses and they get gifts too, so they'll understand. At some level, you simply must face the basic numerical truth of gifts and house space. With every new Christmas, birthday, and special occasion that goes by year after year, the collection of gifts becomes larger and larger. If you were to please everybody's expectations but your own, you would certainly end up buried in gifts. You need to throw some of these things away when it has become clear they aren't useful to you. Especially when they're ornaments, putting them away won't cause common areas to look empty. It will make them look decluttered.

Now, there is the risk of gathering unnecessary ornaments yourself. Think about garage sales, shopping afternoons at the mall and whatnot. We all tend to get a little carried away in the joy of those moments, until we arrive back home and realize we didn't think ahead. So, be it gifts from others or shopping sprees of your own making, you need to discard ornaments on a regular basis. It will be painful to do at first, but once you see the results that feeling will go away. Of course you can keep valuable things you simply can't replace, like souvenirs from special occasions and things like that. Just remember you don't have a row of empty shelves waiting for you, so you must constantly choose what you keep and mostly let go of things that take up valuable room.

The Private Living Room

A slightly similar, albeit more private place you might also have in the house is a private living room on the second floor. This area is one of the most special in the house because it's where the family gathers to spend some quality time together. It is where you and your spouse can talk while relaxing after a long day of work, but it's also a place where kids can play. In fact, it is common for their games to extend into the smaller living room because it is just so close to their rooms.

Even if it feels like it adds extra work to an already big list of to-dos, I would say you must spend a large amount of your energy in setting up this area of the house exactly the way you want it. As an example, I think it's crucial no other rooms in the house feature a big TV screen. I know it's fairly common nowadays to have each individual room equipped with a big flatscreen. But this, in my view, leads people to spend way too much time inside their rooms, over time getting used to doing everything in front of the TV, even things like eating.

Not only does this give the chance for more dirt to accumulate in many other areas of the house, it also spreads people apart at an emotional level. Even in these times; better said, especially in these times, you should keep the house free from being overcrowded with flat screens. Teleworking has made it harder to separate work from entertainment, especially for our kids. Of course, if they still spend a good amount of their classes online, accessing from home, you should give them proper equipment for it. However, that doesn't mean you should give them the option to turn every room in the house into a videogame zone. If you do, they won't care about decluttering the house themselves and their productivity will decrease dramatically.

Aside from visits, make sure all recreational activities gravitate towards this area of the house. That will pull the family together. It will give you all time to hang out and maybe even more opportunity to discuss further decluttering activities.

The Office

The office is a critical area of the house, especially now that a lot of the work we do at our jobs has shifted to a remote format. In some cases, this new format is likely to stay in place indefinitely, which for us has two very important implications:

- Clutter can also build up in more intangible ways. If we work from home, we need to devise a set of rules to prevent work from spreading into all other areas of domestic life.
- The office is often not an individual space. It needs to fit the needs of every member of the house. This is another area to think deeply about in order to find a solution that helps everyone in the house.
- Do your kids spend a large amount of time with their online classes? If so, you need to teach them the importance of having a dedicated area of work. The best way to do this is to show them by example. If they see you quarrel with your own work, they themselves will develop similar habits and problems.

Let us then begin by stating a fact that is true of the home office but should be kept in mind for all other areas as well. It is, as I said at the very beginning, the philosophy of home decluttering in general. Any house, whether big or small, has a limited number of spaces. We fill them up following universal parameters of what goes where and why, albeit with more or less significant customizations of our own. That much is all perfectly okay, at least in theory, but the problem begins when this system isn't fully remembered day to day. In other words, a cluttered house doesn't necessarily come from having a failed system. It often comes from having a good system, but not being able to stay true to it.

In the case of the office, the lesson is very simple: no matter who we're talking about, your spouse, your children, or yourself, try to find a place where you feel comfortable working and organize things in a way that helps maintain working activities as the top priority. In other words, don't arrange things with pure aesthetics in mind because that's not decluttering; that's interior design. Doing it is going to be tempting most of the time and you'll be able to justify it with any number of pretexts, but it's not what you need. Moreover, it might cause you to buy more things, when all you need is the exact opposite.

It's important you all give yourselves freedom to find the right place to work. It doesn't matter whether it's the children or the adults, following the same principle can make a home office look like a veritable co-working area.

In that spirit, here's how you should keep the office clean. If you have enough space for it, try to install two separate desktop tables, one for adults and one for the kids. Don't skim on the desk chairs. You spend a lot of time in them, so if you don't want to develop back problems, if you want your kids to sit in a good position while studying, get good quality chairs. This is not something you can avoid doing on the grounds of trying to simplify and use existing resources. You simply must get specialized chairs for the office. They're a bit of an investment, but one that is well worth your money.

On the desktops, get a good, solid glass panel to cover their surface. That makes tables much easier to clean, which comes in handy because of how much stuff you're going to do on them. Use containers for pens and pencils, get paperweights and all other traditional utensils, but don't overdo it. Some of us get a little carried away when shopping in stationary stores. I mean, who doesn't love buying new, interesting gadgets, fountain pens, and post-it notes for the office? Since I work as a journalist from home, I must admit this is probably my number one hobby. But then I realized how much waste this buying habit generated, and I knew I needed to stop. The fact is a lot of these things remain unused for their entire existence.

So, before you purchase anything new like I did, do a good overhaul of the things you have, check expiration dates and make sure you're not keeping any dry markers and things like that. After you do, you'll certainly find things you need to throw away, but a lot of things will actually fit some needs for which you intended to go shopping again. As a general rule, always check and clean stuff up to find out whether you're keeping something because you truly need it. More often than not, decluttering the home will help you realize you forgot you already bought something, so you don't need to go buying it again.

If possible, get a separate piece of furniture for things like Wi-Fi routers, printers, scanners, and other electronics. Place it as close to the main desktop table as possible. That way you can avoid having to extend cables all over the floor and actually tie them all up in a single bundle. This is also a critical matter when organizing the office because nowadays almost everything we use at work needs to be plugged in. Some things are going to be wireless, but never enough that you can dismiss this concern altogether.

Mail and paperwork also end up in this area of the house. The place where you put your electronics can have a wooden or plastic crate for you to have a roster with everything that arrives. Be sure you keep that roster moving because things never stop coming in and they can pile up very quickly. I have seen offices that were literally carpeted in unopened mail and let me tell you it is not a pretty sight. To keep that from happening to you, having a roster is step number one, but the crucial part is that you check up on things regularly and either move or throw them away as the case may be.

As for books, I think it all depends on how many of them you have. Serious academics will often have several thousand books as a normal thing, but other professions require much smaller amounts, plus you can have many of the books you need in an eBook library to save space. The first thing, then, is to ask yourself what degree of importance books have in your life. I personally find them very important; I have three big bookcases and an entire wall in the office.

The other big concern with books and bookcases is they are very good at catching dust. My advice is to take your daily cleaning routine, whatever it may be, and add the task of dusting the bookshelves every day. That way you'll never find more than a small accumulation of dust each day, and you'll avoid having to dislodge spiders once a month.

* * *

I understand people will have difficulty following these tips because, let us not forget, it is a troubled situation to be in. So don't be too hard on yourself if there are backtracks and errors along the road. Find your pace and use these guiding principles in a way that fits your timeline. Also, try to take this on in a gradual manner. As we discussed in Chapter Two, remember that there is no need to finish all duties in one single day. In fact, that kind of approach can backfire if you're not careful. Set smaller checkpoints and do this in a realistic manner.

All common areas are big and require a group of hands to clean up properly. You will likely have a hard time at the beginning, when you're only just starting to figure out all the things you want to move around and rearrange. But don't despair. Take your time at this stage and, if you need to, spread it out over a number of weeks. After that, daily tidying up for common areas will really be a breeze. The only real problem will come when it's time for a weekly clean. Because of the sheer amount of space you need to cover, it will always be tempting to not do it or do it reluctantly. To avoid that from happening, try to make these weekly rounds a common task you share amongst all members of the family. To make this easier for the kids, put some music on and start dusting off while dancing a little. Help them see that cleaning doesn't need to be a chore if you do it properly and do it in good company.

Key Takeaways

- The two most important functions of common areas are: presenting ourselves to visitors and giving us a warm reception when we arrive home.
- From the foyer to the more private living room of the house, things are similar in the sense that your goal is to keep things simple, dispense with repeated stuff, and regularly use things that are intended only for special occasions.
- Dusting off always comes before using detergents and other substances to clean stuff.

Decluttering Advice

- Make lists of the things that you have so as to have a clear idea of what they are and which of those things you can donate or throw away.
- Common areas are big, so they are one of the best examples of the importance of teamwork for a proper decluttering of the home.

Chapter 8
Outdoor Space

"Change may not occur overnight, but it can"

— Mike Nelson

This subject can vary greatly depending on the amount of outdoor space you have and how enthusiastic you are about it. Some people are more outdoorsy than others, so this is a question you should meditate on yourself. Also, some people live in apartments and have virtually no outdoor space other than a small terrace, that doesn't really have room for much. Either way, the question of where you stand between these possibilities is a matter you must answer before anything else. Aside from other areas of the house that everyone has in their lives, in one form or another, the whole value of this chapter will depend on that answer.

There is a wide variety of spaces that fall in this category, from sunrooms, terraces, balconies and porches, to patios, gardens, and even greenhouses. All of these, whether covered by a roof of some kind or in the open air, are treated differently from proper house spaces. People use them, but often not regularly, even the most diligent of all. Because of this, they all tend to be threatened by a common danger: neglect.

This often manifests in connection with the habit of holding on to things, which we discussed in Chapter Three. In many cases, things that have no place at home, but we feel too guilty to throw away, end up being kept in outdoor areas of the house. This happens especially when these areas are roofed, so they're not affected by the elements. Of course it happens to deposits too, like attics or basements. But once they don't suffice, outdoor spaces are the next best candidates.

People put things there because that way they are easier to forget, while technically they still haven't been discarded; hence the word neglect. For the most part, our goal vis-a-vis clutter in outdoor spaces has to do precisely with this problem. Therefore it can be expected that people who find it easier to let go of things, who can police their possessions more thoroughly, tend to have less cluttered backyards. We shall try and get to that point ourselves by discussing the most generic outdoor areas and the challenges one usually faces in them.

Same as with any other place, the starting point is figuring out what's supposed to be there and what isn't. Once you have that clear, just discard the rest with no remorse. Chances are anything you left out there is not as likely to be important as the things you accumulate inside. Even if certain things you find aren't damaged, just use the same principle: Are they useful to you? If the answer's no, put them in the car and take them to donate when you have time.

Lisa Hedberg

What to do With Rubble

Because they're not barricaded from the exterior, outdoor spaces have much more exposure to winds, rains, and all the things that these carry with them. This makes for a rather heavy accumulation of debris in all their surfaces, from floors to walls, and all the things you put there in the first place. If dust was a major concern inside, the same can be said about the outside. Granted, you don't spend as much time there so it can't affect you in equal measure, but it also accumulates much faster and more densely. To fight this dirt, you'll need more than a superficial sweep.

Start picking up any garbage you may find spread about on the floor, counters, and other surfaces. Some of these things won't be there, though not because you threw them out but because the wind carried them with it. After that's finished, it's time to sweep and mop the floor thoroughly. You'll find that many outdoor areas have rugged surfaces, like for example terracotta tile floors, which are harder to sweep than tiles. Also, these types of surfaces tend to absorb moisture more easily, which means they catch stains permanently, no matter how deeply you scrub them with detergent.

To keep these surfaces looking nice and clean, it is sometimes a good idea to give them some sort of waterproof treatment. For example, you could have sealant applied to them, so you can be sure that if certain hard to clean substances spill onto them, they won't absorb them. This will help maintain a clean look without too much effort on your part. All you will be required to do is sweep and mop, almost as you would with a tiled surface, like a kitchen or bathroom.

So in essence you want to make sure rubble doesn't affect the integrity of any surface so much that it can't be used anymore. Things like oil canisters we sometimes leave in the garage, drippings from a barbecue party, etc. can often leave indelible stains. By putting a protective layer at least over certain strategic areas, this kind of accident won't happen. You'll pick up the debris that accumulates, sweep the dirt, and scrub certain stained areas—all the while feeling confident that you'll be able to remove the stains.

Plants, Vines, and Home Greenhouses

Another big source of debris, in this case self-generated, are the dry leaves and other things that fall from plants we keep in the house. By the way, this can also be a concern to have in mind inside the house. However, patios and gardens on the outside have many more things of this sort, living organisms that are constantly leaving parts of themselves behind. This requires us to be alert, to water those plants regularly, to trim them and take them out in case they die.

It is simply a fact that plants aren't forever, but this isn't a reason to let them die of starvation. Much like we do with other objects inside the house, plants are in danger of being neglected or forgotten out there while we move about living comfortably indoors. For a long time, I used to do just that. I would forget about my plants and let them die out there. I told myself this was normal, just another part of their cycle, but of course it'd have been more accurate to call myself a plant terminator or something along those lines.

In my head, I had this image of beautiful green pots, vines spreading all over the walls or balconies bursting with colors from all sorts of different flowers. Of course, I was romanticizing on the basis of images I had seen in so many housekeeping magazines in the past. Now, there is nothing inherently wrong with doing that, but inasmuch as it didn't quite fit my own personal lifestyle, it represented a problem. That's why I started this chapter by making it clear to you that all issues around outdoor spaces are fundamentally determined by how big they are, both in fact and in terms of their importance in your life.

This, in turn, will give you a ballpark estimate of how much time you spend in the outdoor spaces of your home. It could happen, for instance, that your house does have plenty of outdoor space, but you don't use it that much. Maybe the weather isn't that nice where you live or maybe you just spend most of your time inside. In cases like these, it is best to be consistent with the habits you know you and your family have. If you try to force things, that's when things get out of control and all outdoor spaces become crammed with stuff you don't really use, and you don't even know how they got there. In other words, decluttering outdoor spaces is primarily about preventing clutter in the first place.

Now, provided you do feel enthusiasm for having plants in the backyard or even cultivating a vegetable or two, the situation is different. One of the first things you need to do is establish a list of days to water the plants, trim them, fertilize them, etc. As you can see, it's quite a lot more work than if you decide to leave the outdoors alone. If you and your family want to do this, you need to commit. The plus side is you get to have a pastime that is really healthy and eco-friendly. Having a small greenhouse at home where you plant tomatoes and a few spices can really help reduce groceries a bit, believe it or not. During the pandemic, I was able to feed my family off these things without going out and risking an infection.

Attics and Basements

These aren't outdoor areas, but they tend to be neglected almost in equal measure. Because they are behind closed doors, it is far too easy to go into the basement and pretend everything's in order. You know why we do that? It's because we know it's not in good shape, so we don't feel comfortable being there.

Luckily, organizing the attic, the basement or any other sort of back room is a task we don't need to face as often as, say, cleaning the bathrooms. Just free up a full day once every two months or so, perhaps a weekend in which you're struggling to find something to do, and go at it in depth. Now, if you haven't done this in a while, chances are you don't even know what's in there. If that's your case, put on comfortable clothes, gather all your work materials (duster, broom, vacuum cleaner, etc.) and above all, get some cardboard boxes. This is because you will most likely be throwing away a large amount of stuff, enough that it won't fit in a trash can.

Since these aren't places in an exhibit, you can even leave some boxes there and label them according to their content. Use some boxes to separate what you'll be throwing out, what you think could be donated, and what you want to keep. After you finish this, proceed to dust or, if necessary, to vacuum clean every surface. Then give it some time for all the dust you stirred up to fall on the ground, meanwhile you can double check the things you put in each group of boxes. After a few minutes, get back in there and sweep the whole place.

As for excess stuff that you don't want in the house but also can't put in boxes because you might need them later, you can put them in plastic bags, tupperware drawers, or the very shelves you may have in these rooms. Whatever solution you end up choosing, all that matters is you don't leave anything uncovered because it will get dirty. The only things you should leave uncovered are those you're positive you'll be using regularly, like the washing machine, the ironing table and things like that. Everything else, cover it up one way or another to avoid moths and dust tearing them apart.

Key Takeaways

- The amount and type of outdoor spaces you have under your watch can vary greatly and some people are more outdoorsy than others. Figure out how those apply to you, so you can set up the appropriate plan.
- Outdoor spaces are more prone to catch dust, debris, and even rubble. This is something you will have to fight against constantly, no matter how outdoorsy you are.
- You can have a lot of fun with plants, gardens, and even small greenhouses. Just make sure you get these things only if you're truly committed.
- Stirring the soil and watering plants will vary in periodicity depending on the plants you have. Do some research in order to know what you must do.
- Attics and basements aren't outdoor spaces, clearly, but we can put them in the same category because they tend to be neglected in equal measure.

Decluttering Advice

- If you tend to visit your basement or attic once every year, chances are you need to do an in-depth decluttering round before anything else.
- When you do, make sure you get cardboard boxes to separate, organize, and label everything you have.

Chapter 9
Housework Economy

"It's easy to pick up a book about home management, read along, laugh at the jokes and put the book down again. Translating that experience into a cleaner, more organized home is another matter"

— *Cynthia Townley*

Rounding up the different areas we covered, we have the following:

- The kitchen
- The bathrooms
- Bedrooms
- Common areas
- Outdoor spaces

As I pointed out before, this is a general reference of what every house more or less has, so the whole customization of the principles to your specific situations is a separate question. Housework economy is something that concerns all of us, even if we're kids and we only have one room under our watch, so there's a know-how that you'll need to perfect along the way. There are a million things you can only find out about after having put your hands in the dough, as it were. So don't worry too much about mistakes and readjustments because they are a part of the experience. It's fixing them that you can't afford to avoid.

This is where our first three chapters come in handy, where we try to understand the origin of home clutter, the benefits and traps of space, and the consequences of having an unhealthy attachment to objects. I know it looks and sounds a little too simple when you look at it, but that's exactly how a good system should look: simple and useful. I guarantee you that getting rid of unused things and managing spaces with pragmatism are basically all there is to it in terms of decluttering a home. The very definition you eventually arrive at in terms of your own housework economy is just a more detailed explanation of how you do those two things.

Since you're here, I'm assuming this hasn't happened yet, which is perfectly fine. Let's be clear, you can't just set up a decluttering regime from scratch. You probably have some crises here and there around the house and that is what you first need to look at. By the very act of facing your current crises you will learn about the patterns and habits that people in your family have and how they influence order around the house. Only afterwards can you begin to visualize a system that is perfectly tailored to your needs.

Discipline, Perseverance, and Cunning

Not all of us are the same when it comes to decluttering a home. Some of us have more spare time to tackle these tasks and others can barely make room for them in their tight schedules. Some know very well what they need to do, while others need some time to think and figure out how to solve certain problems. Even if home clutter is well known by all of us, every single case is different, as I said at the beginning of this book. So think about the tips and topics we discussed as a general guidance, but make sure you find your own way of doing things.

But no matter what that personal way of doing things looks like in the end, remember that this isn't supposed to be a one time job. It is a routine you will enter and live with indefinitely, so you have to do it in a way that doesn't stress you out or gets you too exhausted. You should be able to look forward to every new decluttering session and not be discouraged by the mere thought of it. There will be small and big tasks for each day, and some days will be a bit tough, but you must buckle up because the reward is having a nice, tidy house.

To be able to do this, don't let work accumulate. It is relatively fine if you let a day or two go by, especially if you were simply too busy to declutter the house, but try to keep a good pace at all costs. That way you'll have small duties for each day as opposed to big, in-depth decluttering sessions that will take several days to finish.

Another key to save yourself the work is adopting the minimalist style I have insisted on throughout this book. Everything is simpler when you don't have to look after too many things. It helps to be constantly walking around, both in person and inside your head, to check whether you left something you didn't use in more than a year. This minimalist approach, together with a firm determination not to buy more than what you need, will radically reduce the clutter.

We tend to keep lots of objects we do not know where to place, as we have discussed already. But we rarely take the time to realize how much harm that causes to our overall organization. Thus all spaces and rooms of the house end up being a chaotic mash up of things. Left and right, everywhere we look, it would seem we've spent all our spare time accumulating these things without too much thought about the place they'd eventually have in our lives. On the opposite side of that, we find the minimalist approach.

You don't know where to put something? Do you think maybe you've seen it far too many times and thought the same thing to yourself? Well then, why don't you do something about it? Clutter won't just go away if you're a hard worker. That's a big part of it, of course, but all through that process you must engage your mind and think constantly about how you can improve things. Don't just settle for what you see and know how to do. The only principle you mustn't change is staying with the stuff that you need. This is a category that will not stay the same year after year. It will change as your family's life goes on changing. Decluttering strategies must adapt to keep up with that change.

How to Manage All the Lists We've Discussed

It's simple: Split your lists into two types, one for to-do lists and one for observations you wish to implement in the long run. Do the same for every section of the house we've discussed. You can type things in a notebook if you wish, but my advice would be that you try to have this well organized in separate spreadsheets and set alarms on your phone to keep track of them all.

Don't use more tools than you can understand and find truly useful. I've seen many people get cluttered in their own solution before they can even hope to look at their actual problem. If you find that using more than one app is too much, or even if you find that you prefer to use paper and pencil, then do it. I personally think it is better to have things automated, but I understand the tool can become a problem of its own. That shouldn't happen and it is more important you use what you feel comfortable with than anything else.

Now, the number one enemy of lists is that they can start accumulating and overwhelm even the most diligent person. It is a good idea to come up with some plan that makes meeting goals a little fun. You can, for example, promise yourself some sort of reward after every week, so long as you meet the list of things you set out to do in that time. If you are unable to meet those goals, you just move them on to the next week, without any reward and knowing that you will have more to do later on. In the end, that's the strongest motivation you can wish for: wanting to save work for later.

A pleasant way of living in the house does not mean absence of duties; it just means duties are well managed, so you can enjoy and face work in a balanced manner. In this sense, you have a chance to do yourself the biggest of favors by making pragmatic choices. Taking a minimalist approach reduces a lot of the work you would otherwise have to do. We discussed this in a number of ways, every time aiming at the same basic lesson. Don't hold on to things you no longer use, don't buy things you don't need, and don't put things away just because they're too precious for everyday use. These are all recipes for trouble; they increase your work but add no extra value to the quality of life. I know they're decisions we make with that interest in mind, but we must now learn to distinguish and see what's what.

Key Takeaways

- The recipe against home clutter, put very simply: getting rid of unused things and managing spaces with pragmatism.
- There are two phases to the challenge you face: facing the biggest crises you have and afterwards setting up a routine. Of course, these steps should never go the other way around.
- Whether using digital apps or paper and pencil, just make sure your tool for drawing spreadsheets or any other form of blueprint for your plans does not become an obstacle of its own. Use what is most comfortable for *you*.
- Lists should come in two types: to-do lists and observations of things you wish to implement later down the road. In other words, tasks for right now and tasks for later.
- The minimalist approach can be reduced to one single principle: keep only what you need.
- But keep in mind that your life is in constant change and so too will change the things you need. A proper decluttering strategy should keep track of these changes.
- Be mindful of the amount of lists you have and choose a reward so you can motivate yourself to go through them instead of piling them up.

Decluttering Workbook

The Essential Guide to Organize and Declutter Your Home and Life With Exercises and Checklists

"The journey of a thousand miles begins with one step."

— **Lao Tzu**

By picking up this book, you have already taken the first step to a new, more organized, and beautiful life. You must feel proud of yourself for this. I certainly am very proud of you!

The life you dream of is possible, and together, we will make it a reality. Come with me, and I'll show you the way….

Introduction

So, let me guess: you've picked this book up because you just can't bear how cluttered your life and your space feels right now. You've already tried getting the clutter bug under control, but it has been impossible to make any lasting changes. You often wonder, *Am I just a messy person?* When you visit someone's beautiful and organized home, you feel a tinge of envy and admiration: *I wish I could be like them and have what they have.*

You may feel like you're stranded inside a dark tunnel with no ray of light visible anywhere, but trust me: you can turn your life completely around. No matter how bad your clutter is, you can clear it. The thought of living in a beautiful, organized home may feel like an impossible dream right now, but it *can* become a reality for you.

How can I say all this with so much confidence and conviction? Because I know what you're going through; I've been there myself, and I am well aware of how excruciatingly painful it is to be surrounded by clutter.

Introduction

All my life, I struggled with clutter. As a little girl, when I was told to clean my room, I would gather all my scattered toys, shove them in a basket or two, and hide them under my bed. The thing was, I had an idea of what "clean and tidy" should look like on the surface, but I had no clue how to achieve it. My parents told me to clean my room, but there was no instruction on how to go about it. Can you relate to this?

And if you're anything like me, you're also a perfectionist. You want to do everything exceptionally well, or else you just won't do it at all. You've tried to bring your clutter under control, but since you couldn't accomplish all the goals you had set for yourself, you just gave up and resigned yourself to a life of clutter and chaos.

The most valuable piece of wisdom I've learned on my journey of decluttering and getting organized is this: anything worth doing is worth doing poorly. If you haven't cleaned your bathroom because you want to make sure that the toilet is perfectly scrubbed and bleached, the floors are washed, the grout between the tiles is scrubbed—maybe, for once, just start small.

Think of the one thing you can do quickly that will make the biggest difference, perhaps cleaning the toilet. Instead of trying to do the whole bathroom all in one go, just clean the toilet quickly. You can do it in under five minutes. I am not suggesting that you shine it to a sparkle, but a short cleaning session would make a huge difference to how you feel about your clutter problem.

In this book, I will give you clear, step-by-step instructions for getting your space and life organized. If you follow all the steps, you'll get the results you desire! Don't beat yourself up

Introduction

if you don't feel you are doing everything "perfectly." As long as you are taking some action, you are moving in the right direction, and that's worth applauding and appreciating.

I'll give you a mantra that I want you to keep with yourself for the rest of your life. It applies to all areas of life, and it *definitely* applies to decluttering and organizing. *Doing something imperfectly is better than not doing it at all.*

If you can remember this short sentence and truly ponder the great wisdom contained within these few words, you will definitely conquer your clutter and achieve all your other goals in life. A little goes a long way. Even a small amount of progress will compound over time to become a huge transformation.

Take Your First Baby Step Right NOW!

In the first chapter, I'll share with you my formula for setting realistic goals that you can actually achieve. These are the type of goals that make you feel empowered, not the type that leave you feeling inadequate or incompetent.

But first, I want you to complete a task. Why am I asking you to complete a task in the introduction of the book, before we even get to the first chapter?

It's because I want you to start this journey with a win, and this little win will motivate you to take more action because you'll feel a sense of accomplishment right away. You see, in the past, every time you started a decluttering journey, you took your first steps feeling overwhelmed, perhaps even scared. You felt there was a mountain in front of you to climb, and you were quite certain that you'd fail.

Introduction

This time, I want you to start out differently. I want you to feel like a winner. I want you to be proud of yourself for picking this book and taking the first step.

Perhaps you have been criticized and shamed for being a messy person by people close to you who do not understand what you are going through. You have always wanted to change; you just don't know how. I am proud of you because you are not one of those people who indulge in wishful thinking; by purchasing this book, you've proven that you are among a very small percentage of people who take action to change their life.

To help you feel like a winner, here's what I would like you to do: Think of one thing you have been procrastinating on and do it right now. Make sure it isn't anything too big or excessively time-consuming. Perhaps the task for you would be putting that plate away that's been sitting on your desk for a week, or maybe finally putting your clothes in the washing machine. Maybe that task is cleaning your toilet. Just make sure that whatever the task is, it takes you no longer than 10-15 minutes. If you pick anything more time consuming than that, you will start feeling overwhelmed, and then you might spiral downward into a whirlpool of negativity and self-flagellation.

Once you have completed that task, give yourself a pat on the back and reward yourself in some way. Maybe you can enjoy a cup of coffee afterwards, take the time to simply gaze at the sky, listen to your favorite music, or do something else that feels truly good to your soul.

Feeling good is essential on this journey. If you feel good about yourself and your environment, you will automatically be more motivated to keep it clutter-free. Reward is also a

Introduction

much stronger motivator than punishment. By rewarding yourself for the things you do right, you are building new neurons that will get you in the habit of winning daily. Just remember: life is not about the big wins; it's all about the small wins that, over time, add up to become huge transformations.

Now, go and complete that one task you've been putting off! When you're done, reward yourself, and come back to this book tomorrow. And I really mean it: don't pick it back up before tomorrow. Take one step at a time.

This time, you have me holding your hand, and I promise to take you to your goals.

How to Use This Book

Since this is a workbook, I want you to work with it! If you want, you can read all the chapters at once, then come back to Chapter 1 to start working on the exercises. This would help you get an overview of the type of exercises you'll be performing while working through the workbook's contents. The important thing is to go slow but remain steady with your progress.

I am not expecting you to conquer your clutter overnight or even in a fortnight. You didn't create it in a day, after all. It takes time to create change at a deep, fundamental level.

It may feel tempting to skip some of the exercises, but I would caution you from doing so. Every single exercise has been carefully added to this book. It is there for a purpose. Following the sequence in which the workbook lessons and exercises have been presented will help you get the maximum benefit out of this book.

Also, don't forget that simply reading this book won't help you conquer your clutter problem. Change can happen in your life if you regularly put into practice what you learn from this book. Being neat and tidy is a habit just as much as living with clutter is. You are retraining yourself to act, think, and live differently; it's a process that cannot be hurried. Every single exercise aids this process of transformation.

If you are especially eager to get to the decluttering part, it may feel tempting to skip Part I of the book. But don't do that! Even if you manage to successfully apply the teachings of the rest of the book, your chances of rebounding will be relatively higher if you don't build a strong foundation from which to launch your decluttering journey, which you'll do by completing all the exercises in Part I.

Take your time to absorb the material in each chapter and work through one exercise at a time. Don't be in a hurry to get everything done. At the same time, don't allow yourself to procrastinate. Set a daily target of reading at least a few pages every day and complete the exercise(s) contained within those pages.

Stay consistent and persistent. The neat and tidy life you've always wanted to live is within your reach, and I am here to show you the way!

Part One

Preparing for the Transformation

Chapter 1

The Power of Your Self-Image and the Importance of Goal Setting

"You'll never get organized if you don't have a vision for your life."

— Linda L. Eubanks (Abramson, 2019)

I know what you're thinking: you desperately want to remove all the clutter from your life. Must you read a chapter on goal setting? I understand you, and trust me, I felt the same way. I would pick up a book on decluttering and then immediately start getting rid of things. I just didn't have the patience to do what I thought were superfluous things like goal setting and creating a vision for what a decluttered life actually looks like to me.

So what happened every time? I would go through these marathon decluttering sessions. My space would look neat and tidy for a while, but that never lasted more than three or four days. Clutter would make its way back into my life with a vengeance. The next time I would get around to dealing with my clutter, it always felt more overwhelming than the previous experience. I am not too proud to admit that almost every single time I tried bringing some kind of order to my space was when I expected guests over, or when things had turned so bad, I couldn't live another day the way I had been surviving. Maybe you can relate to that.

Over time, I realized that to facilitate any kind of lasting change, I needed to have a clear vision for what I wanted to achieve and then set goals to turn that vision into a reality. Without a vision and proper goals, we are bound to remain caught up in a vicious cycle of decluttering and slipping back into a cluttered existence all over again. I really felt like a hamster on a wheel trying to break free from my clutter. I was focusing too much on the negative instead of the positive experiences I wanted to create for myself. Yes, all I wanted was to get rid of my clutter, but I never gave much thought to exactly what I wanted my ideal space to look like. Does this sound like you?

Another major impediment for me was my self-image. Our self-image dictates every single experience of our lives. We can't change anything in the external world without first altering the self-image from which every life experience springs forth. Trying to change things in the world without altering the self-image that gave birth to it is akin to fighting your reflection in the mirror. If you want to change what is being reflected back to you, then you must make changes to your appearance. There is no point fighting with the reflection you see in the mirror.

If there is just one thing that you take away from this book, let it be what I will share with you about intentionally designing your self-image. If you can master this idea, then you can change every aspect of your life.

Transforming Your Self-Image

So what exactly is your self-image? Simply put, your self-image is the sum total of your ideas, beliefs, and perceptions about yourself. It's what you choose to believe to be true about who you are.

In most cases, a person's self-image has been formed by the opinion of others. Were you told as a child that you are messy? Did you get yelled at frequently for apparently being terrible at taking care of your things and putting them back in place? Were you labeled as being "untidy," "shabby," "clumsy," or other words that don't do much to lift up any child's self-esteem?

These labels and perceptions seep so deep into our subconscious that we hold on to them as the truth, but none of these labels are true. You don't have to live your life being the person that someone else says you are.

> *"Science and psychology have isolated the one prime cause for success or failure in life. It is the hidden self-image you have of yourself."*
>
> — Bob Proctor ("110 Bob Proctor quotes," n.d.)

Who you want to be is entirely in your own hands, and today, you will make a commitment to become the person you have always wanted to be. The only thing standing between you and the person you desire to be is your attachment to your old self-image. Now is the time to let go of it.

While we're discussing self-image in the context of decluttering and becoming an organized person, it applies to every area of life. I would highly recommend applying the principles you learn in this section to every area of life. I can guarantee you would be amazed by the transformation you'd experience.

By creating a new self-image, you can create a new life for yourself. It doesn't matter where you are in life right now or what your past has been like; the only thing that truly matters is where you want to go and who you want to be. Your destiny is entirely in your own hands!

Exercise 1.1

Date:_____

Write down all the words/phrases you believe to be true about yourself. This can include both positive and negative words (for instance: messy, disorganized, always late, fun, gentle, kind, etc.).

Circle all the negative words/phrases and write them down on a separate sheet. On another sheet, note down all the positive words/phrases you believe to be true for yourself. (The second sheet would be like your cookie jar. Whenever you are feeling low, you can read this and remind yourself of all the wonderful qualities you have.)

Now, for each of the negative words/phrases, create a positive affirmation that counteracts it. For instance, if one of the words on your list is "messy," you can write something like, "I am an extremely neat and organized person." Keep in mind that affirmations are always written in the present tense; it's never "I will be…" It's always going to be "I am…" because you want to start believing that what you want has already happened. It is already your truth. Do this for every single negative word/phrase you have on your list. Make sure that you are using a positive word while writing your affirmation. For instance, don't write "I am not disorganized." Instead, you can write, "I am extremely organized; I have effective systems in place for managing my life and my space."

Once you have written positive affirmations for all the words/phrases, take the papers (except the one where you wrote down the positive words that define you) and burn them. You can also just tear them apart and throw the remains in a body of water. As you do so, say this to yourself: "I am lovingly releasing my old self. From this very moment, I am a different person."

Every day, read the affirmations at least thrice: morning, noon, and night. I strongly recommend you do this practice immediately after waking up and right before going to bed, as those are two times of the day when the doors of the subconscious are wide open. Hence, anything you practice during these two moments will have an amplified effect on your life. You also want to read these affirmations every time your mind starts telling you something negative about yourself. It is definitely going to happen because our self-image has been formed over time through repeated words and experiences. It takes time to bring about a complete transformation.

I strongly recommend you continue this practice for at least 90 days. That may seem like a long time, but I can promise you that your life will not remain the same if you can do this for 90 days.

Exercise 1.2

Date:_____

To begin with, you need to have at least one role model who inspires you and whom you can look up to. Find a person you really admire who has the qualities you wish to have in yourself. This can be someone you know in person or someone you have come across online. It can even be a famous celebrity well-known for their work in the decluttering/organizing space. You can also pick more than one person and note down below all the qualities you admire in them.

Thrice a day, spend at least five minutes every morning, noon, and night learning a little more about them and their habits. Visualize yourself as having the same qualities/habits you admire in them.

This is an extremely powerful exercise. Do it every day for the next 90 days, and your life will change for the better!

Setting Goals that Motivate and Inspire You

"All who have accomplished great things have had a great aim have fixed their gaze on a goal which was high, one which sometimes seemed impossible."

— Orison Swett Marden (Pathak, 2021)

If you're familiar with business and management terminologies, then you likely already know about the SMART model of goal setting. In case you are hearing about it for the first time, fret not. I will guide you through the process of setting SMART goals that you actually end up achieving.

According to the SMART model, every goal must be (Wikipedia, 2022):

Specific: You should know precisely what you want to achieve. So if you want a well-organized, super functional space, then exactly what would it look like?

Measurable: The goal should be set in such a way that you can measure your progress over time. For instance, you can take a "before" picture of your space before you start decluttering. Keep a representative picture handy of what you would like your place to eventually look like. It doesn't have to be exact, but close to your vision of your ideal environment. Every week, you can rate your progress based on how far you have come.

Achievable: If you set a goal that doesn't feel achievable, you'll just end up frustrated, giving up as soon as the first challenge or obstacle arises. Your long-term goals can (and should) be very ambitious, but your immediate/short-term goals should be things you truly believe are achievable for you.

Relevant: Your goal should be relevant to your vision for yourself and the life you want to live. If it's not, you simply won't remain motivated to pursue it with consistency. Your goal should also be something that feels realistic to you. For instance, vowing to declutter your entire house in one weekend is simply unrealistic. More likely than not, you'd end up feeling exhausted and depleted if you tried doing it. Even if somehow you managed to achieve it, you'd end up with a cluttered house again because the clutter problem is as much of a behavioral and attitude problem as it is a physical issue. To shun clutter from your life permanently, you need to work from the inside out. Working on your habits, attitude, mindset, and behavior is the most important thing here.

Also, your house didn't get to its present condition in one or two days. It is simply unrealistic to think that you can get rid of it all in just one or two days. You must stay patient and consistent while building a new self and a new life for yourself.

Time-bound: It is important to set a timeline within which you intend to achieve your goals; otherwise, there simply won't be any sense of urgency to take action. Your goal date should not be something too far into the future. You may modify the date as you get closer to it, but do your best to always achieve your goals within the timeline you have set for yourself.

Decluttering Workbook

Exercise 1.3

Date:_____

Write down two decluttering goals: one for this week and one for this month. For instance, your weekly goal might be to declutter one specific corner of your bedroom. Your monthly goal might be to finish decluttering the entire bedroom.

Be sure to write down your goals on paper. Research shows that people have a much higher chance of achieving their goals when they write them down.

Every week, review your progress and set a new goal for the forthcoming week. Once you get into the habit, I want you to also start setting quarterly and yearly goals for yourself. But for now, just focus on setting weekly and monthly goals. If you try doing too many things simultaneously, you'll start feeling overwhelmed, and you simply won't make any progress.

Once you've written your goal down, write down all the steps you would have to take to achieve it. Of course, you can keep modifying the steps as you make progress, but you need some kind of a rough plan to begin with. Without action steps, a goal isn't a goal; it is merely wishful thinking.

Take a piece of thick paper and cut it to the same size as your ATM card. Write your goal on it with a tentative date by which you are planning to achieve it at the top. Keep this card with you at all times; it will keep you focused on what you want to achieve. You can also place the card in a protective plastic cover (like the ones used for keeping name tags safe).

Read your goal every morning, noon, and night to make sure that it seeps deep into your subconscious mind. Every night, write down at least five action steps you will be taking the next day to achieve your goal. The key to having a successful day lies in planning it properly the previous night.

Every day, do the things that you dread the most first. This way, you'll build your confidence by fostering a sense of achievement early on in the day.

Chapter 2
Getting Your Vision Crystal Clear

"Don't let others tell you what you can't do. Don't let the limitations of others limit your vision. If you can remove your self-doubt and believe in yourself, you can achieve what you never thought possible."

— Roy T. Bennett, *The Light in the Heart*
(Goodreads, n.d.)

Setting a clear goal for what you want to achieve and the self-image you want to build that complements this goal is the first step toward turning your dream life into a reality. The next step is to turn this goal into a reality in your mind's eye through visualization. The clearer your vision of exactly what you want to achieve and who you want to be, the easier it will be for you to remain focused on your goals. This vision should motivate and excite you so that you take consistent action towards your goals on a daily basis.

Whenever you are feeling unmotivated, you'll bring this vision to the forefront of your mind, and it will provide you with some much-needed motivation to keep moving forward.

Every person's vision for what they want their life to be like, who they want to be, and how they want to live their life will be different. In this section, I'll give you all the important points you need to consider while creating your unique vision.

> *"Vision without action is merely a dream. Action without vision just passes the time. Vision with action can change the world."* –Joel A. Barker (Brainy Quote, n.d.)

Ideal Self-Image Vision

What if you don't know exactly what it is you desire? This is a problem many people have. The interesting thing about decluttering your space is that it affects your mind in ways you wouldn't have deemed possible. Just like how you discover a favorite item that's long been buried under the weight of so much unwanted clutter, you discover that layer after layer of *mental* clutter will start falling away. Once you have gotten rid of all unwanted excesses, you will discover your unique vision for life. It all starts with decluttering your space! The snowball effect happens across all aspects of your life.

But the question is, what should you do for now? Doing the introspective work laid out in the exercises here will definitely help you develop clarity on what you truly want. You can also ask the people closest to you to learn more about yourself. If all else fails, just pick a person you truly admire, observe how they live their lives, and follow suit. Modeling success is often the best way of becoming successful yourself.

As you start intentionally focusing on a vision, you'll develop greater clarity on whether or not that vision truly resonates with you. Also, keep in mind that your vision is not set in stone. You can keep modifying it regularly; your vision may change as you grow. It is important to accommodate those changes whenever necessary.

Exercise 2.1

Date:_____

As I said earlier, your experience of life depends upon the person you are and the person you choose to be. Now, I want you to think about your ideal self—the self you have always wanted to be.

Answer the questions below without restricting yourself in any way. Don't think about how it will never happen or how far away you are from being the person you would like to be. Think of it as a Christmas wish that has already been granted to you. All things are possible, so answer these questions with complete honesty.

   1. What does your ideal self look like? What are the predominant thoughts, emotions, ideas, and perceptions of this person?

2. How does this ideal self show up in daily life? What does this person wear? How does this person behave? What kind of body language does this person display?

3. What kind of daily routine does this person have that supports them in being the person they are?

Exercise 2.2

Date:_____

These questions will help you identify what is working for you in your life. Once you know what these things are, you can simply choose to do more of those things and less of the things that don't leave you feeling amazing.

1. If you had a meeting with a very important person, how would you present yourself? (For example, wear your best clothes, do your hair and makeup, etc.)

Decluttering Workbook

2. What is different on the days when you are feeling on top of the world? (For instance, do you take out your special China, soak in the bathtub with candles in the background, set the table properly, etc.) I want you to come up with a list of things you do that make you feeling amazing. Don't brush anything off as trivial; what helps you feel good is important. It doesn't matter what anyone else thinks.

3. What are your most prized possessions that you save for special occasions? Make a list of all those things that you believe are meant to be used only on a few occasions.

Ideal Lifestyle Vision

If you want to get rid of your clutter problem once and for all, then you need to know exactly what kind of space you want to be living in. You must also have a clear vision of the kind of lifestyle you want to have.

Exercise 2.3

Date:_____

Think of your ideal living space and your dream lifestyle to answer the following questions:

1. Describe your ideal living space using five adjectives that best define it.

2. What is the décor like? (Is it classic, modern, vintage, minimalist, or something else?)

3. Who is living with you? Or are you living alone?

4. What are the predominant colors that you see around you?

5. What kind of lighting do you have in your living space?

6. How big is your space?

7. How does your space make you feel?

8. How do you begin your day?

9. How do you end your day?

10. What kind of activities and hobbies do you regularly engage in? (For instance, do you spend most of your time in your home office? Do you cook lavish dinners? Do you create artwork?)

11. What does your daily routine look like?

12. What kind of self-care/self-love rituals do you practice every day?

13. What are your favorite items that bring joy to your heart?

Exercise 2.4

Date:_____

Create a vision board by making a collage with images representing your ideal self and desired lifestyle. You can cut out images from magazines, or you can look for images on Pinterest and then print them out. Select only those images that truly speak to your heart and inspire you. If you don't want to print them, then you can just create a digital vision board and use it as your desktop or phone background. Ideally, it should be someplace where you'll be viewing it several times a day. If you decide to print the pictures, make sure that you have them displayed on a poster board. You should hang the board on a wall that you face most often throughout the day, like the wall opposite your work desk.

Chapter 3
Your Habits Reveal a Lot About You!

"Clutter is the physical manifestation of unmade decisions fueled by procrastination."

— Christina Scalise (Abramson, 2019)

I'm sure you know at least one of those people who seem to instinctively and intuitively know how to stay organized. You can grill them as much as you like to find out their secret, but all you'll ever get is, "I don't know. I just do things the way I do." They aren't lying. In most cases, they are really clueless about why they are the way they are— just like you can't quite figure out why you have a clutter problem while others don't. My biggest issue with many of the popular decluttering books on the market is that they seem to have been written by born organized people. They don't empathize much with a person who faces the kind of challenges you and I do. Do you know what I am talking about?

People like you and me feel a strong desire to become organized, but we feel clueless about where to start—and, most importantly, how. For a "born-organized" person, the answers to these questions come naturally. We need a clear sense of direction, guidance, and precise instructions for bringing order to our world.

Fret not; I understand you. I was exactly like you for a very long time. It's only when my life became unbearably dysfunctional because of my clutter problem that I decided I needed to turn over a new leaf. I spent a long time researching and experimenting with different systems. In this book, I will share all my discoveries with you and the system I eventually developed for myself.

Yes, you really need a system for staying clean, tidy, and functional. I wish I could wave a wand and transform your life in an instant. I really do know how much it hurts when you feel burdened with endless piles of clutter. You walk through life feeling jaded and exhausted. Unfortunately, there is no magic wand. You'll have to do the hard work, but with the methods, techniques, and system in this book, you are definitely going to succeed. Just stay consistent and be patient with yourself; even the smallest amount of progress is worth celebrating. Any improvement is better than no improvement.

Born-Organized vs. So-Called "Messy" People

What exactly is the difference between a born-organized person and someone who has been labeled as "messy" and "disorganized?"

"Laziness is nothing more than the habit of resting before you get tired."

— Jules Renard (Brainy Quote, n.d.)

The greatest difference lies in their habits. Organized people have consciously or unconsciously managed to establish successful habits. Becoming successful is not an event; it is a process built on the solid foundation of daily habits.

I've spent a lot of time studying the habits of organized people. I felt a bit embarrassed once I started taking notes and began comparing their habits with my own. But before I tell you more about those habits, let's take a fun quiz to find out where you stand on this habit spectrum right now.

Answer each one of these questions with complete honesty. I know it can feel awkward and embarrassing to admit some of these things, even to ourselves, but if you want to take a quantum leap from where you are to where you'd rather be, you must first have an excellent understanding of exactly where you stand at this moment in time.

The Habit Analysis Quiz

So here we go. Think about each of these questions and circle the right answer in complete honesty. No wishful thinking here; only an honest assessment is allowed.

1. Do you leave your towel on the bed after taking a shower?

    Yes/No

2. Do you wait until the last minute to start packing your bags before a trip?

   Yes/No

3. When you return back from a trip, does it take you several days/weeks/months to fully unpack?

   Yes/No

4. Are you often late for appointments?

   Yes/No

5. Do you refer to yourself as a "messy" person?

   Yes/No

6. When you're cooking, do you put everything away before you sit down to eat?

   Yes/No

7. Do you hit snooze every morning and go back to sleep?

   Yes/No

8. Do you always wake up late and feel like the day has slipped by?

   Yes/No

9. Do you often feel overwhelmed by everything you need/want to do?

   Yes/No

10. Do you struggle to get back to work after what you intended to be a short break?

    Yes/No

11. Are you often struggling to find things at the right time when you need them?

    Yes/No

12. Do you have too many single socks in your drawer?

    Yes/No

13. Do you have piles and piles of clothes but nothing to wear?

    Yes/No

14. Does the idea of doing laundry intimidate you?

    Yes/No

15. Does your living space turn into an even greater mess every time you come back with shopping bags from outside?

    Yes/No

16. Do you dread stepping inside your bathroom?

   Yes/No

17. Do you often turn your underwear inside out and wear them for a few more days because you don't have any clean underwear left?

   Yes/No

18. Are you often buying too many of the same things because you can't remember where you kept the original item?

   Yes/No

19. Do you often feel like crying because there is so much clutter and chaos around you?

   Yes/No

20. Do you feel your life and home has spiraled out of control?

   Yes/No

21. Do you feel bogged down every time you step back into your home?

   Yes/No

22. Do you leave things lying around after completing an activity?

Yes/No

23. Are you someone who never picks up after themself?

Yes/No

24. Do you leave closets/cupboards/drawers open when you leave the room?

Yes/No

25. Do you feel you look like a mess all the time?

Yes/No

26. Do you feel embarrassed about your appearance when you accidentally bump into someone important?

Yes/No

27. Do you dread having guests over?

Yes/No

28. Would you go on a cleaning overdrive if guests were to come over tomorrow?

Yes/No

29. Do you feel housework is meaningless drudgery?

Yes/No

30. Do you say "yes" to everything when it is practically impossible to complete all the tasks you have loaded onto your plate?

   Yes/No

31. Do you struggle with saying "no" to people when they ask you to do something?

   Yes/No

32. Do you get up and just start your day with zero planning or forethought?

   Yes/No

33. Are you often tripping over your own clutter?

   Yes/No

34. Do you feel burdened by the things you own?

   Yes/No

35. Do you save your best clothes, China, and other items for special occasions only?

   Yes/No

36. Do you remain in your PJs until afternoon or much later in the day?

   Yes/No

37. Do you look in the mirror and think about what a mess you are?

Yes/No

38. When you are trying to get your place clean, do you often stuff things in a corner—"out of sight, out of mind?"

Yes/No

39. Do you really *want* to live in a clean and organized home but have no clue how to do it?

Yes/No

40. Do you feel lonely in your battle with clutter and chaos, as if no one understands you and what you are going through?

Yes/No

How to Calculate Your Score

Give yourself one point for every "yes," then tally the final number. Here's what your score says about your habits:

0-5: Well, you are already a very well-organized person. You likely don't need this book, but you can always pick up a few more tips and tricks to level up your game.

5-10: You aren't doing too bad! Forming a few more systems for managing the various aspects of your life will help greatly.

10-20: You feel disturbed by the clutter and chaos surrounding you in some areas of your life. You really want your space to be more functional and efficient but aren't entirely sure how to do it. Well, this book is for you. By doing a little work on yourself, you can become tidier and more productive.

20-30: Alright, you are really struggling with your clutter. Hang in there. I've got your back. This book is for you, my dear! I know it seems impossible to believe that one day you'll be able to live a clutter-free life. May I even suggest that someday, people will be inspired by your example? They'll ask you the same question you have when you come across a super-organized person: "How do you do it?" Trust me; you'll get there. I've got your hand, and I am going to lead you there.

30-40: Houston, we have a problem! My heart goes out to you, my dear. Trust me; I was exactly like you. I felt my entire life was spiraling out of control. Every day of my life was an impossible race against time, and every night, I went to bed feeling defeated. I had so much clutter and chaos around me that, at times, I felt I would cry. Well, there were times when I actually did cry. I wanted nothing more than to live in a beautiful, organized home. At times, that dream felt so far out of reach—but, hey! I finally did achieve my dream, and so will you. For now, you just have to trust me and allow me to lead you on to a new life. If I can do it, so can you! Consider this paragraph to be a warm hug from me. I feel your pain, and that's why I'm here to help you. Buckle your seatbelt because you will experience a dramatic transformation, and it will happen sooner rather than later.

Part Two

Getting to the Root of Your Clutter Issues

Chapter 4
Clutter is Essentially Decisions You Are Procrastinating On

"Clutter is the physical manifestation of unmade decisions fueled by procrastination."

— Christina Scalise (Postconsumers, 2020)

Prior to working as a financial journalist, I worked for a finance company. As was frequently the case, I had once again missed an important deadline. I started working late and couldn't finish on time. My boss was annoyed, and after a long lecture on how I needed to improve my non-existent time management, he asked from the other end of the telephone line, "Look around your office right now and tell me: what is it like?" I went white and silent in embarrassment. To provoke an answer, he interrogated further. "Is it messy or organized?" I whispered as if I was scared to hear the answer myself. "Messy." "I knew it!" he said with exasperation. Then he planted a seed in my mind that has continued to grow since that day. He said, "Your environment is your mind. Clear the clutter if you want to do your job properly! Not just the clutter in your office but also in your home and all your personal spaces, but at least start with your desk and your office. You can't think or plan clearly when sitting at a cluttered desk."

Now *that* was a big idea! I hadn't thought of my personal space and the clutter inhabiting it in those terms. This conversation happened a very long time ago when a mentor I deeply admired had taken me under his wing to work for him and learn the nitty-gritty of the business from him. He really cared for me and thought I was exceptionally creative and original. The only issue was that I needed to become organized, proactive, and disciplined. He did his best to guide me as much as possible, and I valued every word that came out of his mouth as rare gems of wisdom.

Today, I am sharing this idea with you. I have definitely come a long way since those enlightening words fell on my ears. However, it didn't happen in a matter of days or even a year or two. To fully incorporate the wisdom of those words took me several years. But that's because I did not have a workbook like this in my hands that could guide me to take all the steps I needed to take. I knew I needed to get my act together, but the "how" part left me baffled and clueless.

The thing was, my boss was one of those born-organized people. He knew how to keep his mind and environment clutter-free. He could tell me what I needed to do, but he did not understand the struggles of a person who doesn't know how to organize and stay tidy. If you follow all the instructions in this book, then I can promise you that you can accomplish within a few months what took me years.

To begin with, just remember this mantra: *your environment is your mind.* You can't think clearly and calmly in a cluttered environment. Observe your environment, and you will definitely see how the state of your physical space corresponds with your mental state.

Defining Clutter

The word "clutter" is derived from the Middle English word "clotteren," which means "to clot" or coagulate. In other words, clutter happens when there is a blockage or stagnation. No wonder being surrounded by clutter feels like a heavy weight on the soul! Every time we manage to get rid of things we no longer love or that no longer serve us, we feel like a heavy weight has been lifted off our shoulders. We suddenly feel lighter and happier. I'm sure you can relate to that.

In the ancient Chinese art of *feng shui*, this is exactly how clutter is defined. Clutter accumulates as a symptom of what is going inside you. When you feel stuck, indecisive, depressed, or just plain negative, you are prone to accumulate clutter. The catch is that clutter attracts clutter because stagnant energy produces even more stagnant energy. It becomes increasingly hard to feel positive, happy, motivated, and productive in a cluttered environment because the stagnant energy accumulated around you in the form of clutter affects your mental state.

Now, you may be inclined to dismiss *feng shui*, but just think about your relationship with clutter, and you'll realize there is a lot of truth in this ancient Chinese art of harmonious living.

Different Types of Clutter

By now, you have a fairly decent idea of what clutter really is. Let's define it further so you can have set criteria for screening all your belongings to check for clutter. Clutter can be classified as:

Those things that you no longer love or value. Have you ever walked into a beautiful home or maybe even a shop where every object was carefully kept in a specific place? How did you feel being in that space? I am sure you felt uplifted, delighted, and energized.

Now, think about the most cluttered, shabby, and untidy room you have ever been inside. How did that feel? You felt drained, tired, and negative, right? If you take away just one thing from this book, let it be this: surround yourself *only* with the things you love, value, and cherish. Anything else is too large a burden to bear because it is clutter!

Things left in an unfinished state. Anything left unfinished in your environment represents an issue that you haven't dealt with in your life. This could be anything from the painting sitting on your easel for over a month without any set date for getting back to it to the leaky faucet in your bathroom.

Every time you successfully attend to these physical manifestations of unfinished businesses, you'll feel lighter and relieved. I'm sure you know what I am talking about!

Anything kept in a shabby, disorganized, or untidy state. This ties in with the first point we discussed, that clutter is anything that is not loved or valued. Now, it is possible that you *do* love and value your things but aren't showing them the respect that they deserve. You allow them to remain in a shabby, disorganized, and untidy state even though they mean quite a lot to you. In that case, they just become clutter. You may feel joy when you are using them, but they feel like a burden at other times. Eventually, this may wear them out much faster than they are supposed to be used, or perhaps you'll acquire more of the same things because you're never able to find them when needed.

This is why decluttering and organizing go hand-in-hand. You must start out by decluttering. Thereafter, you must stick to a plan for organizing and staying organized. Don't worry; we'll address both of these aspects through this workbook. For now, I just want you to understand that keeping even your favorite things in a shabby, disorganized, and untidy state can make them feel like clutter. This doesn't mean you have to get rid of your favorite things. Definitely not! You just have to organize them and learn to take good care of them. This way, they will serve you and bring joy to your heart for a long time.

Too many objects crammed into a small space. Sometimes a place isn't necessarily disorganized but feels cluttered simply because there are too many objects in too small a space. This can happen when your life or family has grown, but the size of your home has remained the same. The best solution would be to either move to a larger space or rent a storage space where you can store some of your less frequently used items. If you don't have that option, then you can either pare down your belongings or work on smart storage solutions that maximize space. Thinking creatively becomes absolutely essential here.

Smart storage solutions are great for maximizing space, but even this works only to some extent. There comes a point where you feel like you just can't breathe smoothly and freely in a space like that.

Exercise 4.1

Date:_____

I highly recommend you write down the answers to the following questions in the space provided here. Yes, you can mentally answer the questions, but writing has a powerful impact on developing clarity of mind and purpose.

Look around your space and ask yourself the following questions:

1. What are the objects you love/value/cherish the most?

2. Are you taking good care of these objects and showing them the love they deserve?

3. Is your place clean, or is there dust accumulating everywhere?

4. Is your space large enough to accommodate all your belongings?

5. If you neatly organized your space, would it be able to comfortably contain all your belongings?

6. What are the things you no longer use or need?

7. What are the things you should definitely give away to someone else who may find them useful?

For now, I just want you to start building the muscle to start recognizing clutter. Later on, I will give you a battle plan to deal with it all. A problem half-understood is a problem half-solved. So don't take this exercise lightly!

Procrastination Lies at the Root of it All

According to the Merriam-Webster dictionary, procrastination means "to put off intentionally and habitually." Simply put, it is a decision not to deal with things in a timely manner.

How often have you thought you'd start working on the report tomorrow, fold the laundry later in the evening, or put away the grocery bags "at some point?" The more tasks you keep piling up on top of the ones you already have lying around, the greater your clutter problem.

Making decisions in a timely manner requires us to deal with the emotions that arise at the idea of doing something we perceive as unpleasant or cumbersome. It's not that the task is unpleasant or cumbersome—but somewhere along our experiences in life, we came to *associate* it with drudgery.

I have tried many methods of dealing with procrastination. For me, Mel Robbins' five-second rule works the best. In her own words, "The five-second rule is simple. If you have an instinct to act on a goal, you must physically move within five seconds or your brain will kill it. The moment you feel an instinct or a desire to act on a goal or a commitment, use the rule. When you feel yourself hesitate before doing something that you know you should do, count 5-4-3-2-1-GO and move towards action."

Every time I am procrastinating on something, I just do a countdown from five to one, get up, and do what needs to be done. Honestly, it isn't always easy—following the five-second rule does require a certain amount of commitment—but if you stick with it, then it works like a charm. So when I think, *I'll fold the laundry later on*, or, *I'll put the food containers away once I've finished eating my dinner*, I do the countdown and just get things done. Of course, there are certain things that can't be attended to immediately, but you need some kind of a system for managing those tasks, as well, so that you aren't constantly procrastinating on them. In Parts III and IV, we'll delve deep into the system and methods you need to maintain a clean, tidy, and organized space.

For now, just make a commitment to start implementing the five-second rule in your life.

Exercise 4.2

Date:_____

1. Set an hour aside and write down all the things you have been procrastinating on.
2. Pick at least three things from this list and get them done today.
3. Keep adding to this list and regularly review it. Every day, pick three things and get them done. If you have several huge tasks that require a few days or weeks to complete, you can have one big task scheduled for several days and add two small tasks that can be completed in a single day.
4. Whenever you are struggling to take action and do what needs to be done, use the five-second rule. Do a countdown, "5-4-3-2-1-GO," and just take action!

Chapter 5

Your Perfectionism is Keeping You from Living a Neat and Tidy Life

"People always try to be perfect. That's why they don't start anything. Perfection is the lowest standard in the world. Because if you're trying to be perfect, you know you can't be. So what you really have is a standard you can never achieve. You want to be outstanding, not perfect."

— Tony Robbins (AZ Quotes, n.d.)

The root causes of procrastination are a deep-seated fear of failure and an obsession with perfection. As the quote above suggests, perfectionism truly is the lowest standard in the world because it prevents you from achieving anything as you continue putting off starting. You can't be successful at something you never started. On the other hand, you're able to give yourself the satisfaction that you haven't really failed since you didn't start in the first place.

Sit back and think about it for a moment. Are you one of those people who claim to be an "all or nothing" personality?

Are you either going to do something outstandingly and exceptionally well or not at all? And those times when you must get started eventually, do you put off doing things until the last moment because you're afraid you'll get a better idea later and you want to give your absolute best to the task at hand? The way this pans out is that you end up doing things at the eleventh hour—perhaps you pull off one or several all-nighters. You feel you are racing against time; it causes you tremendous stress and maybe even leaves a few dark circles under your eyes.

The question is, does this kind of mindset really support you in the long run? Can you achieve more by delaying things until the last minute? Maybe such a strategy can work up to a certain extent, but you would never realize your full potential and achieve the level of success you desire with such a chaotic approach.

The Cure for Procrastination: Just Get Started

As a reformed procrastinator, I can share with you a mantra that has helped me beat all procrastination. It's a quote by G. K. Chesterton: "If a thing is worth doing, it is worth doing badly" (Society of Gilbert Keith Chesterton, 2012).

I am not suggesting you shouldn't strive to give your absolute best to the task at hand. Far from that, I am suggesting that there is never going to be a perfect time to get started. The potential each human being has for growth and self-improvement is infinite. You will never "arrive" in the truest sense of the word because no matter how far you go, there will always be a new level for you to achieve and conquer. It may sound terribly cliché, but the journey is indeed the reward! But if you never get started, you will never achieve anything. You'll remain stuck in a cycle of failure because you aren't trying to achieve success at all.

I am not suggesting you should not strive for constant improvement, but refinement and modification must happen naturally. At some point, you must just dive in and publish that paper you have long been improving upon or start that exercise regime you have intended to begin but never actually got around to starting. When the desire for improvement becomes an excuse for remaining paralyzed in a state of inactivity, you are only pushing success further away.

The question is, how can you overcome this situation? Again, the five-second rule really helps here. Just think of something you must get done and take the first step. Something very interesting happens once you take the first step: you suddenly develop the motivation to take the second step, the third step, and so on. It is usually the first step that's the hardest. Taking the first step is akin to half the battle won. So just get started!

If you are anything like I was, another issue you have is that you think you'll get started once you have a proper plan. After all, you wouldn't want to take the first step in the wrong direction, right?

I have come to realize this is just another good excuse to keep procrastinating. You don't have to know every single step of the way; you just need a clear picture of the goal you want to achieve and the first step you must take right now. When you take the first step, the second step will become clearer. After the second step, the third step then becomes clearer, and so on. You just have to keep moving forward, and the path will illuminate itself. Just try it. You'll definitely become convinced this is *exactly* how it works.

"The journey of a thousand miles begins with one step."

— Lao Tzu (Brainy Quote, n.d.)

Exercise 5.1

Date:_____

Think of something you have been procrastinating on and write down below how it is making you feel. Record all the negative emotions you're feeling as authentically as possible.

Now, write down the first step you must take to complete this task. You don't have to complete the task; just complete the first step right away.

Once you have completed the first step, write down how you are feeling.

I am sure you'll feel relieved and relaxed as if a weight has been lifted off your shoulders. Next time you find yourself procrastinating on something, go back to your journal and read how you were feeling before completing the first step and how you felt after it. Ask yourself, what is better? How would you really like to feel?

I am sure this will motivate you to take the first step. After taking the first step, it would become easier to continue taking the next step. As long as you are moving forward, you are getting closer to your goals. Don't be too hard on yourself; it's okay to go slow. The only thing you can't do is give up!

I would caution you from reading any further without completing this exercise. Don't allow yourself to procrastinate on it; otherwise, you won't get any real benefits from this chapter. Transformation happens only when you are consistently taking action. Without applied action, knowledge doesn't have much power. Your mind may tell you, *I'll do it after reading the entire chapter, I'll do it tomorrow,* or *I'll do it later,* but don't listen! You are just adding more items to your list of things you are procrastinating on.

Just complete this exercise and then come back to the next section. Go on; do it *right now*!

How to Take Consistent Action and Stay Productive

Nothing frustrates me more than when I am told to do something without any proper instructions on how to actually do it. I'm sure you can relate to that! I know I told you to go and complete the first step for something you are procrastinating on. I also told you that you must consistently take action to keep moving toward your goals. Easier said than done, huh? You are afraid that despite your best intentions, you'll get sidetracked and start procrastinating again. Perhaps you'll convince yourself you are taking a ten-minute break, then procrastinate on getting back to work. To help you remain productive, I am going to introduce you to one of my favorite methods of time management: the Pomodoro Technique!

Now, what on earth is this pomodoro technique?

The technique was developed by a man called Francesco Cirillo. It involves working with intense focus and zero distractions for a period of 25 minutes. At the end of 25 minutes, you get to enjoy a short five-minute break. When the break is over, you get back to work for another 25 minutes. Each 25-minute period of productive work is known as a "pomodoro," which is actually the Italian word for tomato. Cirillo named his time management method the pomodoro technique because the original kitchen timer he was using as a university student to time his work looked like a tomato (Cirillo, 2018).

After completing four pomodoros, you can enjoy a long 20-minute break. After the break, simply repeat the process all over again. You'll be amazed by how much you achieve by practicing this method. Indeed, I find this the best method for staying highly productive throughout the day. Anyone can do anything for 25 minutes; it doesn't sound too hard or eliminating. It is also easier to convince the mind to remain focused for a short duration of 25 minutes than practicing the same for several hours in one go. The mind loves seeing a finishing line; it makes everything seem easier to manage.

You can get your own timer and set it up manually for each pomodoro. Alternatively, you can set up an account on a pomodoro tracker website like the one at pomodoro-tracker.com. By creating an account, you can track your progress throughout the day and review how productive you have been over an extended period of time. At the end of each pomodoro and after each break, you'll be alerted by an alarm.

I recommend that you use this technique not only for your decluttering and cleaning projects but also for other important things. This has been an absolute game-changer for me, and I am sure you'll also see amazing results.

Some rules to keep in mind while using the pomodoro technique:

- Pick one task and focus completely on it.
- Be sure to eliminate all distractions. (No checking messages on your mobile phone or clicking on your inbox, unless it is an essential part of the work you are trying to do.)
- If someone interrupts you for something while you are in the middle of a pomodoro, tell them you'll get back to them in a while. Make a note of their request and address it later on when you have time.
- Pausing or ditching the pomodoro shouldn't be an option you avail of regularly. It should be done only under rare circumstances when it is absolutely necessary to address the unexpected request right away. In that case, I recommend abandoning the pomodoro altogether and starting fresh. The online tool allows you to hit the pause button, but I would recommend not using it. It is better to start a new pomodoro and work for the entire duration of 25 minutes. The only situation in which you can hit the pause button is if you are absolutely sure you won't need any more than 60 seconds to address the unexpected request. Any longer than that, and you'd be better off starting a new pomodoro. Just don't count the abandoned pomodoro when calculating your long break.

- At the end of 25 minutes, take a break, even if you feel like you want to complete the task you are engaged in.
- During the break, don't sit at your desk or do anything mentally demanding like answering important emails. Instead, take a break to recharge and refresh your body/mind. Take a short walk, do some light stretching, drink some water, use the restroom, etc. To stay productive throughout the day, it is very important to move the body at regular intervals.
- Get back to work the moment the alarm goes off. Don't procrastinate or dilly-dally, or the method just won't be effective.
- You can check your email and messages during the long break, but avoid sitting at a desk or remaining glued to the screen. It is better to do something refreshing like a little exercise, having a healthy snack, spending time with your loved ones, etc. Again, make sure that you aren't prolonging the break once the alarm goes off.
- If you finish your task before the 25-minute period is over, you can simply continue the pomodoro by doing another important task. Just make sure that you continue working without a pause.

Exercise 5.2

Date:_____

Start using the pomodoro technique today (or tomorrow, but don't put it off for next week or another time—remember, we are training you to start overcoming the habit of procrastination and perfectionism).

Set the clock for 25 minutes and start decluttering. Don't pause or stop until the alarm goes off. I would recommend doing just one decluttering pomodoro every day as a habit. Any more than that, and you risk feeling overwhelmed. Yes, you can do a decluttering and cleaning/organizing marathon once a week and do as many pomodoros as you like on such days, but as a regular part of your routine, it is better to have only one pomodoro for decluttering/tidying every day.

You can keep another pomodoro for cleaning. Of course, if you have a large house and a fairly big family to look after, you may need more pomodoros for cleaning, decluttering, and tidying. Use your judgment to schedule your pomodoros in a way that best suits your needs and lifestyle. My advice of staying on the conservative side is geared toward a busy executive who already has too much on their plate to take care of. Staying consistent is far more important than having occasional spurts of productivity every couple of days.

Also, start using the pomodoro technique to stay productive throughout the day. It's perfect for managing all types of work, not just cleaning and decluttering tasks. Come on, now; give it a go! You'll definitely feel good about yourself after you realize how much you can achieve in a short duration of 25 minutes.

Chapter 6
Habits of a Neat and Tidy Person

"We are what we repeatedly do. Excellence, then, is not an act, but a habit."

— Will Durant (Brainy Quote, n.d.)

In Chapter 3, we discussed how our habits determine our success or failure in every area of life. Your life is the way it is because of your current habits. You can't change your life without first transforming your habits. That super neat and tidy person you wish you were like has intentionally or unconsciously established a strong set of habits that support them in maintaining the kind of lifestyle they are enjoying right now. You don't have to be born a neat and tidy person to become one. Incorporating the right process, methods, and techniques can enable anyone to get the desired results.

In this chapter, I'll share with you the kind of habits you need to build if you want to become neat, tidy, and organized. I'm not suggesting that you have to do it all in a day; that would only cause pain and frustration. Instead, pick just one or a handful of habits to begin with. Once you have succeeded in consistently practicing the habits you have adopted for at least a week, you can adopt a new one and start working on it. Just remember, practice always makes things better.

Also, as you are building these new habits, be sure to remain patient with yourself. Building new habits requires dismantling the old dysfunctional ones that no longer serve you. This is a process, not an event. It takes time.

According to a study published in the European Journal of Social Psychology, on average, it takes at least 66 days for a behavior to become an automatic part of one's psyche. The study also showed that it takes anywhere from 18 to 254 days for a new habit to be formed (Clear, 2020).

Think of your efforts as wet clay. It takes time to bake them in the sun so that they can become robust pieces of pottery. It would be highly unrealistic to think that if you decided to adopt a new habit, it would start coming naturally to you immediately. In the beginning, you'll have to put in a lot of conscious effort—just like how you were so attentive when you started learning how to drive. Now, you can drive without giving much thought to what you are doing. You know you have successfully formed a new habit once you can practice it without thinking about what you are doing.

Pick Up After Yourself

This is undoubtedly where you need to begin your habit-building journey: start picking up after yourself! If you are dealing with clutter and mess, you are most likely one of those people who leave the towel lying on the floor after stepping out of the shower. You get dressed and walk out of the room, leaving the closet door open. You come back from the grocery store and leave the products lying on the kitchen counter for days, never giving a home to your purchases. Does this sound like you?

From now on, I want you to build new habits. Put things away right after you have completed a task. Don't just shove them out of sight, but let them rest in their proper home. I'm sure you have heard the saying, "A place for everything, and everything in its place."

From the biggest to the smallest object, everything should have a proper place in your home. This way, you aren't scampering all over the place to find things at the last minute. You know exactly where you will find what you are looking for because you have intentionally placed it in its home. Of course, we haven't reached the decluttering and organizing section of this book yet, so it's okay that you aren't abiding by this mantra for now. Right now, I just want to familiarize you with the concept of giving a proper home to every object. Even after you start decluttering, it's not going to happen right away. It will take you time to start living in a home where there's a place for everything, and everything is in its place.

For now, it's enough if you can start picking up after yourself and putting things away after you have used them. If you don't have a proper place for things, you can use a shelf or a basket to put items of a similar type or category together.

Here are some suggestions for how you can start practicing this habit today:

- Hang your towel in a place where it can dry after showering.
- While cooking, put tools and containers back in their place right after using them. Avoid sitting down to eat until you have finished putting everything back in place.
- When you arrive home, be sure to bring only a few bags in at a time. Put all the items away then and there. Bring the other bags in only after you have put away the bags you brought inside. You'll be amazed by how relaxed you feel when you aren't drowning in a sea of shopping bags after coming home.
- Close all drawers, closets, and cupboard doors every time you leave a room.
- Whenever you leave one room, pick up some items that don't belong in that space and place them where they need to go. Get in the habit of constantly assessing what you can take with you in your hands before you're ready to walk out of any room. I find this to be a powerful habit to remain neat and tidy. It only takes a few moments to assess what doesn't belong in a particular space and carry it to another space, and you were going there, anyway.

Exercise 6.1

Date:_____

Look around you. What are the things that shouldn't be around you right now? Select at least five of these items and put them away. Do it right now!

For the rest of the day, do your best to keep picking up after yourself. Continue the practice tomorrow, as well. Before going to bed, set the intention that you are going to stay tidy by picking up after yourself. Setting your intention the night before is a powerful tool for having a productive day. Don't just do it in your head; write it down in a digital or paper journal before falling asleep. This way, it sinks deeper into your subconscious mind, which dictates most of your behavior and thought patterns. If you can stay consistent with it, you'll eventually notice significant changes in yourself and in your life.

For tomorrow, set the intention right now by writing it down here.

Use The 20/20 Rule

The 20/20 Rule is another life-changing concept I learned from The Minimalists' Joshua Fields Millburn and Ryan Nicodemus. According to this rule, whenever you are struggling with decluttering decisions, it is best to let go of the thing you are undecided about if the following two conditions can be met (Fields Millburn & Nicodemus, 2019):

- You can replace the item for less than $20.
- The item can be easily replaced in less than 20 minutes.

Now, I am not suggesting that this can work as a panacea for all your decluttering items—of course not! Some items may cost less than $20 but are special to you for sentimental reasons. Maybe you can replace something in less than 20 minutes, but another copy of the same item just won't feel the same to you. As with anything else, you have to use your judgement here. The 20/20 rule is a great tool to have in your toolbox that may prove useful while making certain decluttering decisions.

Let me give you a few examples of where I applied it in my own life:

- I had 15 coffee mugs sitting on my kitchen shelf when I didn't even drink coffee. None of the mugs were particularly aesthetically pleasing to me, so it just didn't make sense to keep any of them.
- I had more than two dozen cheap $10 t-shirts bought on sale. I didn't like any of them, and they got treated like trash, but I had bought them simply

because they were cheap. We'll talk more about the importance of always surrounding yourself with the things you truly love and value later on in the book. For now, I am just giving you examples of the kind of things you can begin to remove from your life. You are worthy of the clothes that make you feel like a million dollars, not low-quality discounted pieces that you find hard to value and care for.

- The worst places for collecting other people's junk are yard sales—or the modern-day version, Facebook Marketplace. Since everything is so cheap (after all, someone desperately wants to get rid of it), we end up buying things that mean nothing to us. Now, I'm not saying that you can't discover an occasional treasure in someone else's junk, but even the most seasoned yard sale enthusiast would admit that those instances are quite rare. My love for buying cheap items on sale led me to buy too many things that I didn't need at all—case in point, a collection of history books I kept around for two decades, never opening a single one of them. I was keeping them for someday when I may read them. I had to admit that such a day was never going to come, and if it did, I could easily buy those books from a second-hand store at a low price.
- Wasn't I the queen of duplicate kitchen tools? Did I really need 10 potato peelers? What was I planning to do with 20 can openers when I always reached out for just that one?

These are just some examples of things I decided to get rid of. Your list may look similar, or it may be completely different.

Either way, I am confident that you'll benefit from practicing the 20/20 rule to whatever extent you are most comfortable.

Exercise 6.2

Date:_____

You don't have to immediately start getting rid of things. I wasn't ready for it when I first started decluttering. This is where my "command-Z" solution comes to the rescue.

For now, you can place the things you think you should get rid of in a special cardboard box and put it away. Place it somewhere out of sight. If you start missing any of those items, you can easily rescue them. It's like hitting the "ctrl" + "z" buttons on your computer keyboard to undo your last action, hence, the name, command-Z solution.

You can easily undo the act of discarding by rescuing any items you miss since they are still around in a cardboard box. However, most of the time, I don't miss those items. The saying "out of sight, out of mind" tends to be quite true for these types of items. But it is better than taking an extreme step like fully discarding an item when you are not ready to do so. If, after a long time, you haven't missed any of the items that are there in the box, you can go ahead and discard those things.

Get Better at Prioritizing

Most people who struggle with clutter are very bad at prioritizing. Picture this: you decide to finally scrub the walls of your bathroom. You collect all the cleaning supplies and get down to business. Suddenly, the phone rings—it's your mom calling. She asks if you'll join her for coffee this afternoon. You drop everything and start getting ready to go grab coffee with your mom.

I am not suggesting that you form a super rigid schedule with no room for flexibility. That would be just as extreme as not having any schedule at all. What I am suggesting is that you start weighing in on the demands placed upon you on a daily basis and the work you already have on your calendar. Of course, you'll have to start scheduling things in advance on your calendar. We'll discuss more about it in the next section.

Let's look at two scenarios and the different choices you may make:

Say your mom lives close by, and you regularly see her. She casually asks you to grab coffee with her, and you agree even though you have guests coming over in three hours, and your house and bathroom aren't ready to receive them. Since you meet your mom regularly, you have to prioritize here. Preparing your home for the guests coming over is more important than grabbing coffee with your mom on this particular afternoon.

In another scenario, let's say that your mom lives in another city. She is visiting you for a few days and wants to make the most of your time together. Hence, she suggests that you both grab coffee together. In that case, scrubbing the bathroom shouldn't be your priority, as you can do it another day when your mom won't be around.

You have to consider your priorities moment to moment and from situation to situation. The answer is always going to be subjective to you and your goals. The only thing I am suggesting you stop doing is saying "yes" to everything! Your friend calls you up and asks if you'd bake cookies for her son this afternoon, and you say yes. Your father asks if you will pick up his clothes from the dry cleaner this afternoon, and you say yes. Your husband asks if you'll arrange a dinner for his boss and colleagues this evening, and you say yes. Your friend wants to talk to you about her recent breakup with her ex, and you know very well the conversation would go on for at least two hours, and you say yes.

Just look at the number of things you have said yes to! Aren't they going to leave you feeling overwhelmed as if you're racing against time, trying to stretch yourself to impossible limits?

If you want to organize your physical space, then you have to start by organizing your mental space. Everything outside is a reflection of what is inside. To become organized, you have to become really good at assessing what is the most important thing for you to do right now and then focus all your attention on that task. Of course, the answer will be different from moment to moment.

Exercise 6.3

Date:_____

Write down below the most important thing you should be doing right now. Focus all your energy on doing that task. Maybe right now, the most important thing for you is reading this book. In that case, give your full attention to what you are learning here and vow to implement it. It is only through

Decluttering Workbook

practice that you fully imbibe the knowledge you want to acquire.

Whatever the answer is for you right at this very moment, just make sure that you are devoting 100% of your attention and energy to it right now. Record your answer here.

Plan Things Ahead of Time

I used to be one of those people who woke up without a plan and just attacked the day. No wonder I used to get sidetracked every time an unexpected request came up! I would drop everything to attend to it because I didn't have a proper plan for sticking to whatever task I had at hand.

The best time to start planning your day is the night before. You want to have a vision for how you would like the day to go. It's important to think about the tasks you'll be performing. If you have any appointments, meetings, or any kind of time-bound activity, it must be written down. In the digital age, it's very easy to set a reminder to make sure you get prompted at the right time to show up for your engagements.

Another thing that used to waste a lot of my time was standing in front of the refrigerator, wondering what I wanted to cook. Once I decided what it was I wanted to make, I would try and gather the ingredients, only to realize that I was short on several items. I would run to the grocery store to buy those ingredients only to come back and realize I had forgotten two other things I needed. It took me a long time to understand the importance of writing things down and making proper lists.

These days, I plan the menu for the week every Sunday. I look at all the recipes I plan to make that week and then check my grocery supplies, noting down all the ingredients I need to buy for the week. This makes life a lot easier, and a trip to the grocery store goes by much faster. After all, I am not getting distracted and sidetracked by the plethora of options available at the store. I know exactly what I need, so I stay focused while shopping for groceries. I also vary the menu for the week depending on how busy I will be and how long it would take to prepare each meal. For instance, on those days when I have several work meetings and numerous errands to run, a crockpot meal works better for me. On days when I have a lot of free time to spare, I can afford to prepare a much more indulgent dinner.

You really need to think about your day and assess how busy or free you will be. There are two ways of planning your day: on an hour-to-hour basis or simply having a checklist of things you intend to accomplish on a given day. Personally, I prefer the latter, as trying to schedule every minute of my day really stresses me out. Instead, I keep the list with me, and every hour or couple of hours, I check to see which task I am ready to tick off. Doing the hardest thing on the list first (or at least early on in the morning) really helps in giving me a sense of accomplishment.

Exercise 6.4

Date:_____

Buy yourself a physical planner that looks good and is aesthetically pleasing—or use a digital one with nice features. It's essential that you enjoy the layout and overall look of the planner, as this will increase the chances of you actually using it.

Here are the things you want to plan the night before:

- **Create a To-do List:** Write down all the tasks you want to accomplish. Classify them as P1, P2, P3, and so on based on priorities, with P1 being the highest priority, and P2, P3, etc. as lower priority.

- **Do the Most Important Task First:** Set the intention of completing the highest priority task first thing in the morning. If that's not possible for some reason, then do it as soon as you can. Don't start your day with the easiest tasks; that just increases your chances of procrastinating on the most important task.
- **Decide What You Will Wear:** Think about the activities you'll be performing and decide your outfit accordingly. Check the outfit to make sure that it is clean and wrinkle-free. If not, do whatever needs to be done to prepare it for the next day. Don't put off things like ironing your outfit for the next morning. Life is so much more peaceful when you can take a shower and quickly slip into your outfit for the day. The same goes for the shoes you'll be wearing. I would highly recommend that you wear shoes at home; this really increases productivity. We'll talk more about it in the next chapter. Just make sure that your shoes are also appropriate for the day's activities.
- **Review Your Menu Plan:** I would recommend that you plan your menu on the day you intend to go to the grocery store. This would be every couple of days or maybe even daily for some people. For others, going to the grocery store is a viable option only once a week. Every night, review your menu plan for the next day and think about the time it will take to prepare those meals—or if you'll be buying them, how long it will take to place your order and receive it. You need to have a plan for how you'll fit meals into your schedule. Sometimes, you may have

to switch the meals around if an unexpected demand on your time comes up.

- **Write Down the Timing for All the Important Appointments/Meetings:** You can plan your day on an hour-to-hour basis. I would not recommend it, as I personally find it overwhelming, but if that works better for you, then give it a try. I would recommend simply writing down your list according to priorities and adding only time-bound tasks to your calendar. For instance, if you have a meeting with a client or your son's teacher at 2 PM, write that down. Any task that must be completed at a specific time should definitely be listed on your calendar. I also strongly recommend that you set a reminder using any of the digital apps. This way, you'll be prompted before the meeting/appointment, and missing it just won't be an option for you.

Part Three

Decluttering for Life

Chapter 7

Start with YOU!

"The thing that is really hard, and really amazing, is giving up on being perfect and beginning the work of becoming yourself."

— Anna Quindlen (Mackey, 2022)

So you're ready to conquer all the clutter in your life, but there's so much of it that you don't even know where to begin sorting it all out. Where should you start? My answer is always "start with yourself."

Decluttering or organizing your home isn't the end goal. The *real* end goal is to live in a home that supports you in living a peaceful and beautiful life. What matters most is for you to love yourself and your life. At the deepest, most fundamental level, clutter is a manifestation of your lack of love for yourself. We surround ourselves with an excess of cheap discount-store items we don't really love simply because we don't feel worthy of regularly using the things we truly like. It is difficult to take care of things we don't love or truly appreciate having. And when we fail to care for our surroundings properly, we start berating ourselves. Very soon, the guilt and self-loathing set in, and we remain perpetually trapped inside this vortex of negativity.

The only way to break out of this vicious circle of suffering is by loving yourself first. I know a lot of you are going to squirm at this idea. Isn't it selfish to take time out for yourself when you have a family to tend to? My dear, let me remind you of something: you can't fill anyone's cup from an empty pitcher. To be able to fully support your loved ones, you have to first give yourself all the love and support you need.

Once you start loving yourself by taking better care of your body, mind, and soul, everything else will fall in line. You'll automatically want to live in a clean and organized home. When you feel well put together, you automatically want to put your environment in order.

Loving Yourself is the Master Key to Living a Clutter-Free Life

You must be thinking, *Do we really need to discuss how to love ourselves? Isn't that something all of us know instinctively?* Unfortunately not! Just start paying attention to the constant chatter inside your head, and you'll realize that the way you talk to yourself is so awful, you wouldn't talk like that to even your worst enemy.

The voice inside our head isn't really our own voice. It's a voice we acquired from the authority figures in our early childhood. This voice tells us things like, *You aren't good enough, You always mess things up, You just can't get anything right, You're such a failure,* and the list goes on and on. When you came into this world, you were an innocent little baby. You loved all parts of yourself. I'm sure you have seen how lovingly babies play with their feet and hands. There isn't an ounce of self-loathing or self-criticism in a baby. But as the baby starts growing up, they are constantly bombarded with harsh criticism and verbal attacks.

I am not suggesting that parents, teachers, and other authority figures do this intentionally; of course, they don't. They do it with the desire to help the child and simply because they do not know any other way. This is how the authority figures in their life conditioned them, and they have subconsciously adopted this as the only "right" way to treat a child. But you have this book now, and I am here to teach you a better way. It doesn't matter how much you have grown up; your inner child is still there deep inside your heart, just as hungry for love, support, and compassion as ever before.

The best part is that I'm not just going to tell you to start loving yourself. That sounds all fluffy and nice, but how do you actually put it into execution? In this chapter, I will offer you several practical ways in which you can start practicing self-love and self-care.

And you don't have to start practicing all of it at once. The last thing I want is for you to crash and burn in an attempt to practice self-love. As always, the most important thing is to take baby steps. Adopt just one thing at a time. Once you get comfortable doing one thing, add another, and so on. Don't let your perfectionism (the whole "all or nothing" approach) fool you. One small step at a time is better than trying to jump the entire hallway in one leap. Start small but stay persistent; that's the only way to be successful at anything in life!

Your Self-Love Mantra

In eastern spirituality, a mantra is a phrase repeated often so that it seeps deep into the subconscious mind. Since the subconscious mind dictates our reality, repeating a specific mantra can transform our experience of life. If you have ever been to a yoga class, then you might have wondered why the students and teachers chanted "om" before, after, and perhaps even during the class. The word "om" is a mantra that affects the mind at a very deep subconscious level. Anyone who uses it knows that, at the very least, it relaxes the mind and relieves stress. To make this journey into greater self-love easier for you, I want to initiate you into a self-love mantra. This is how I started my own journey, and I want to pass on this knowledge to you.

I realized that the main reason I had a clutter problem was that I did not love myself enough. Inside my mind was this constant chatter about how I wasn't good enough, I can't do anything right, I am messy, I am disorganized, I can't get my act straight, etc., etc. No matter how hard I tried to change my external actions, nothing would work until I changed my inner dialogue.

In order to counteract the chatter, I created my own mantra. With every inhalation, I would say quietly inside my mind, "I love myself." With every exhalation, I would say, "Deeply, profoundly, dearly." Whenever I started feeling anxious or the negative thoughts became overwhelming, I would focus all my attention on my breath and repeat this mantra.

I want you to start using this mantra from now on. Whenever you find yourself engaging in any kind of negative self-talk, take your focus off the negativity and put all your concentration on your breath. Repeat this mantra quietly inside your mind. Over time, it really starts working its magic. At first, you repeat the words, but you may not believe what you are saying. However, there comes a point through repetition where the words sink very deeply into your subconscious mind. Your subconscious starts believing the words, and eventually, your behavior begins to align with the words you have been repeating.

I'm not suggesting all this can happen in days or even weeks. It takes time for a major shift to occur, but the process of transformation begins the moment you take the first step towards bettering your life. Just try it, and I am sure you'll feel a difference. If nothing else, use it as a tool to distract yourself from negativity, especially in those moments when negative thoughts seem to completely overpower you.

Exercise 7.1

Date:_____

Put this book down for a few minutes and practice the mantra I just taught you. Shift your focus to your breath. With every inhalation, say to yourself quietly inside your mind, "I love myself." With every exhalation, say to yourself, "Deeply, profoundly, dearly." Allow your body and mind to relax fully. Let all thoughts melt away into pure love as you repeat this mantra with each inhalation and exhalation.

Get Dressed Every Morning

This can mean different things to different people. So picture this: how would you dress if you had an appointment or a meeting with someone who is very important to you? You'd put in some effort into looking put together, wouldn't you?

What happens when you make an effort to look presentable and put together? You feel happier and more confident, right?

Don't you deserve to feel this way every single day of your life? Please don't tell me you are so busy that you don't have time to make any effort to look good. As a loving friend, let me say this to you: you deserve better!

You deserve to look good and feel good. We always have time to do the things that are important to us. I am sure if you kept an account of every single hour of your day, you'd find time slots you can spend investing in yourself instead of watching TV, playing games on your phone, or mindlessly browsing the internet. We all do unproductive things, and I'm not asking you to eliminate all such activities from your list. I am simply asking you to prioritize self-care. You are worth the time and energy it takes to look good every day. Your day automatically goes better when you feel good inside, and this is reflected in how presentable you are on the outside.

If being fully dressed for the day implies wearing makeup and jewelry on a daily basis, then start doing it. If, for you, being put together simply means wearing a crisply pressed shirt and skirt, then do that. The whole point is to do whatever makes you feel good, and do it every single day without fail. It baffles me that people put in so much effort to impress the people they do not even like while being their sloppiest and worst around people who are truly important to them, including themselves.

Exercise 7.2

Date:_____

Before going to bed tonight, pick out your outfit for tomorrow based on the activities you'll be performing. Make sure your clothes are clean, tidy, and pressed. Lay them out neatly or keep them on a separate hanger. Getting dressed every morning should be a delightful experience as if you had walked inside a luxury store and found the clothes thoughtfully laid out for you to put on. You deserve this luxury every single day of your life.

Fix your hair and face tomorrow morning. Put in every effort to look and feel your best. You truly deserve it! Do it not because you are going to meet someone special, but because you will be spending the entire day and the rest of your life with the most important person in the world: *you*!

Wear Your Shoes Around the House

So this is a productivity hack I learned a long time ago from *The Sidetracked Home Executive*. The authors recommended getting fully dressed every day, right down to the shoes.

If you're like me, you may just cringe at the idea of wearing shoes that have traveled everywhere outside indoors. To solve this issue, I keep a separate pair of shoes that I only wear indoors. When I'll be spending the entire day indoors, I prefer to wear lace-up shoes. This way, it isn't easy for me to take them off and laze around.

Wearing shoes every morning sends a powerful signal to your brain. The moment you put on the shoes, your mind receives the message that it is time to go to work. You are making a statement to your subconscious mind—it's time for business!

Try this out, and I am sure you'll feel a lot more productive throughout the day. I count this as one of my most life-changing hacks, and I'm certain you'll feel the same way once you've tried it out.

Exercise 7.3

Date:_____

Tonight, set aside a pair of shoes that would go well with tomorrow's outfit. Make sure that the shoes are suitable for all the activities you will be performing the next day. If you'll be spending time both indoors and outdoors, then you may want to have two separate pairs of shoes. You can choose slip-on type shoes you can easily get in and out of if you are concerned about the time it may take to change into another pair of shoes. If you can manage wearing lace-up shoes at least indoors, then I would strongly recommend it. If you don't have a pair, it's a good idea to invest in one. It's not easy being lazy when you're wearing lace-up shoes. Trust me on this one!

Start Using Your Best Things

If you have been drinking tea from a chipped cup, wearing tattered t-shirts to bed, or eating two-week-old leftovers, it's time to remove all these things from your life. Yes, these are the types of items you need to declutter from your life ASAP. You deserve better.

Okay, I get it; your mind is revolting right now. How can you get rid of these things? These are like backups that prevent you from spoiling your precious China or that gorgeous nightgown you bought in France. By eating two-week-old leftovers, aren't you saving yourself time and money?

While using these things may seem practical, they don't leave you feeling good. Hence, they should be eliminated from your life. If you have ever been to a truly luxurious place, didn't you feel like a million dollars because everything around you looked and felt so high-quality?

Why can't you turn your home into such a place? I really feel you deserve it. The only question is, do you feel the same? If not, why? You appreciate such a space when it was created by someone else. Why can't you create such a delightful space for yourself? I'm not suggesting you start buying Mink vases or Van Gogh paintings. The greatest luxury is that of a neat and tidy house, but that goal can only be achieved when you surround yourself with the things you love.

The things you love don't necessarily need to be expensive; they just need to be things you truly value and want to look after. I'm sure you already have quite a few such items. They are most likely stored in the corner of your closet where nobody can touch them, including you. Most people save their best for someday special. They forget that there is only one life we've all got to live. There's no time to put off living for another day. You've got to make the most of every single day!

Think about it: if a very important person were to come over to your home, wouldn't you pull out all of your best things to make them feel comfortable and loved? Aren't you the most important person in your life? Don't *you* deserve to be treated like that special guest?

From now on, I want you to treat yourself like royalty. Start believing that you have been born into a royal family. Every day and every aspect of your life must be completely royal. You deserve to live an elegantly royal life! All the clutter will automatically disappear from your life once you adopt this attitude because clutter is simply an excess accumulation of things that are unloved, unwanted, unappreciated, or not looked after.

Exercise 7.4

Date:_____

Make a list of all your "treasures," including everything that's truly valuable to you, big and small. Pick one item from this list and start using it in daily life. Focus on making every day special instead of waiting for special occasions to celebrate life.

Start Going to Bed on Time

I was really bad at this, and I still struggle with it, if I'm honest. I would often wait until the last minute to complete important tasks. This meant things kept accumulating, and then I would have to do a marathon to complete the task at hand.

I was accustomed to going to bed late at night, and a lot of times, I would pull an all-nighter to complete a pending task with a fast-approaching deadline. This meant I was never well-rested. Every morning, I would hit the snooze button and try going back to sleep. Life felt too overwhelming to deal with. By the time I woke up, it would already be 8 or 9 AM. I felt like I had no control over my life. Worse than that, when I looked in the mirror, I felt awful about the darkness under my eyes. I was barely able to function throughout the day because I was always so exhausted.

The greatest act of self-love and self-care I adopted into my life was to start going to bed on time. Of course, the first night I tried doing it, I just laid wide awake in bed. Instead of going to bed at 1 or 2 AM, I was trying to fall asleep at 10 PM. Obviously, that wasn't going to work. You can't expect the body to adapt to such a radical change on such short notice.

Instead, it's better to gently acclimatize the body over the course of a few days and weeks. So the next day, I tried a different approach: I went to bed half an hour earlier than usual. I did that for a couple of days until I started falling asleep naturally around that time. Once I had established that routine, I reduced the time by another half an hour. I kept repeating the process until I reached my ideal bedtime.

Waking up on time is easier if you go to bed on time. I also prefer to set my alarm on an actual alarm clock instead of on my phone. I find it a much gentler way of waking up; I don't wake up and immediately start staring at a bright screen that pierces my eyes. It also prevents me from checking my phone first thing in the morning, another practice I strongly recommend you give up on. When you start your day by checking your emails and messages, you're allowing the world to dictate how your day is going to go.

Read your plan for the day before starting any activity in the morning. Spend the morning doing things that nurture your soul and give you a sense of groundedness. This should include practicing your self-love mantra, performing your morning cleaning and tidying chores, some form of exercise, and any other activity that recharges your batteries.

You're probably dreading the idea of cleaning and tidying every morning. Don't worry about it; I'll share powerful tools to help change your attitude about cleaning. You'll also learn how to incorporate chores into your routine such that they don't feel like drudgery to you. We'll get to it later on in the book. For now, it's enough if you can start going to bed and waking up early.

How early should you wake up? I really can't dictate that to you. You're the only one who can assess what time is right for you to wake up. You need enough time to start your day on your own terms, to get dressed and put yourself together before you start performing other tasks. The amount of time required for this will be different for everyone, and you need to figure out what works best for you.

Just make sure that you are gentle and patient with yourself. If you're accustomed to going to bed at 2 AM, then setting a goal to wake up at 5 AM starting tomorrow isn't going to be a good idea. Instead, start going to bed half an hour earlier than your usual time and waking up early by half an hour to an hour prior to your usual time. Gradually, keep reducing the time to a point where you reach your ideal sleeping and waking schedule.

Exercise 7.5

Date:_____

Assess how much time you need each morning to perform the activities that nurture your body, mind, and soul. Be sure to account for the amount of time you need to get dressed properly. Set the intention of going to bed half an hour earlier than your usual time, and try to wake up half an hour earlier tomorrow. Place the alarm clock far away from your bed so that you'll have to get out of bed to stop the alarm. If possible, use a physical alarm clock to wake you up in the morning instead of the alarm clock on your phone.

Chapter 8

Kickstart the Decluttering Process

"Don't let the perfect be the enemy of the good. Lower the bar. Actually spending ten minutes clearing off one shelf is better than fantasizing about spending a weekend cleaning out the basement."

— Gretchen Rubin (Hage, 2021)

There are four important terms you need to understand now: decluttering, tidying, organizing, and cleaning. While all four of these terms are closely related, they represent four completely different activities and ideas. Tidying implies "having everything ordered and arranged in the right place" (Cambridge English Dictionary, n.d.). Organizing involves arranging things in a systematic order. Decluttering, on the other hand, involves removing those items from your personal space that no longer serve you or aren't needed anymore. Cleaning is the process of removing unwanted substances such as dirt, infectious agents, and other impurities from an object or environment (Wikipedia, 2022).

In order to live a satisfying life, we have to practice all four regularly. But as a beginner, you don't want to try doing all four together, or you'll burn out and crash. You must begin with decluttering as it is much easier to organize, tidy, and keep clean the things you truly value and cherish than it is to try and practice these methods on items that feel like a burden to you.

Begin with Decluttering

To begin the decluttering process, pick an area of the house that bothers you the most or where you find yourself spending the maximum amount of your time. For me, this area was my bedroom. I decided to start the decluttering process from my bedroom because getting this one room of the house in order would provide me a safe harbor to retreat to every night. Whenever I felt tired of dealing with clutter all day, I could enter my peaceful nest and feel grounded again.

This plan worked out really well for me. So many times during the decluttering and organizing process, I felt overwhelmed. I needed a temporary relief from the chaos that surrounded me. I would make myself a hot cup of chamomile tea and rest on my beautifully made bed, flipping through pages of beautiful homes featured in my favorite home decor magazines.

Ever since I was a little girl, I dreamed of living in one of those beautiful homes where every object radiates with beauty. Somehow, this dream always eluded me. At least by then, I had gotten my bedroom to look aesthetically pleasing, if not exactly like the bedrooms in my favorite magazine. I strongly recommend you pick an area of your home that bothers you the most and that could also serve as a recharging space for your soul.

To start decluttering, first, take every single item out of the space. To make this less daunting, you may want to divide the entire space into several small spaces. For instance, if you are starting in the bedroom, you can tackle the closet in one go. You can also do one shelf at a time, but that may end up taking you too long. You can also perform the decluttering process according to categories.

Under no circumstance should you try decluttering more than one room at a time. For instance, don't try to declutter the kitchen and the living room in one day; that would be too overwhelming. Go slow and steady, tackling just one space at a time.

You are the best person to decide what works best for you. However, if you are unsure, doing your closet first could be a good start. We've become accustomed to acquiring more things than we need or even value in today's times. We buy clothes from discount racks, wear them once, and then those clothes just sit at the back of the closet, completely forgotten.

There is another advantage to tackling the closet first. If you can get your closet to look and feel good, containing only those items you truly enjoy wearing, you'll also feel good about yourself. Wearing clothes, shoes, and accessories that make you look your best provides an instant confidence boost. Dressing up provides the motivation to be more productive. I mean, just try having a super-productive day sitting around in your PJs with unwashed, uncombed hair. You can maybe pull it off for a day or two when you are dealing with a major deadline, but it is hard to stay productive with a sloppy appearance on a daily basis.

Exercise 8.1

Date:_____

Identify the space with which you want to begin the decluttering process. Choose a small area and take everything out of that space. Don't do any more than one room at a time. Make sure that you remove all the items from that space at once for the next exercise.

How to Decide What to Keep and What to Let Go Of

If you're anything like me, it's not enough for you to hear that you must decide what to keep and what to let go of. You need precise instruction on how to arrive at such a decision.

For me, going by my intuition is very important in this process. As I hold each item in my hand, I pay close attention to what I feel. Does it evoke a positive emotional response in me? Am I feeling happy, cheerful, delighted, proud, pleasured? Or does it feel like a burden—something that evokes a negative memory or emotional response in me?

The next thing I ask myself is how I feel about taking care of it. Do I want to take good care of it and treat it with the respect it deserves, or is it going to be tossed around carelessly everywhere? I try to keep only those items I want to take good care of. This is a strong indicator of what I truly value and what isn't so valuable or important to me.

Now, you may be wondering about things like cleaning supplies. You don't feel any particularly positive emotions as you hold them in your hands. For such things, you'll have to consider the value they add to your life. How do they make you feel once you have used them to clean a particular space? If you feel good about any cleaning supply, then it is clearly a keeper. This is how you must assess all your possessions primarily used for utilitarian purposes. Think about the end result you achieve with them, and that should help you decide what to do with them.

Also, with things of a utilitarian nature, proper storage can make them feel like less of an eyesore. When we get to the chapter on organizing, we'll discuss storing your cleaning supplies and other utilitarian items in a more aesthetically pleasing way.

Exercise 8.2

Date:_____

Hold each item in your hands and ask yourself:

- How am I feeling? Am I feeling happy, cheerful, delighted, proud, pleasured? Or does this item feel like a burden, something that evokes a negative memory or emotional response in me?
- Do I want to take good care of it and treat it with the respect it deserves, or is it going to be tossed around carelessly everywhere?
- For things of a purely utilitarian nature, focus on the results they help you achieve and the feelings those results evoke in you. Are those emotions positive or negative?

Decluttering Boxes

For the decluttering process, you'll need four boxes. Mark them as "donate," "alter/fix," "discard," and "ponder." As you go through your clutter, decide whether you want to keep each item. If not, you have to decide which box it should go in.

The donation box will contain all the items that no longer serve you but can prove useful to someone else. The alter/fix box will include all the items that can be fixed or altered—for instance, the shirt you haven't been wearing because of its missing buttons. You feel good wearing that shirt, but the missing buttons prevent you from reaching for it. The discard box will contain all the items that aren't useful to you anymore, and that won't help anyone else, either.

The last box, ponder, is for all those items that you aren't sure about. It is part of the command-Z strategy I shared in Chapter 6. You place all the items you don't use but aren't quite ready to part with in the ponder box. You pack the items carefully to prevent damage and store the box away. If you start missing any of the items in the box, you can go ahead and retrieve them.

Since you keep the box around, undoing the idea of getting rid of that item is easy. If you miss the item, you've established the fact that you truly do need it. But trust me, you won't be needing most of the items you end up storing in this box. I am speaking from experience, and you'll agree with me after finishing all the work we are doing in this workbook.

Exercise 8.3

Date:_____

Get four large boxes and mark them as "donate," "alter/fix," "discard," and "ponder. Go through each item using the questions from the previous exercise and decide which box is appropriate for each item.

You Can Pause, But Don't Stop

When you are looking at heaps and heaps of stuff around, it can be hard to believe there will ever come a point when you've finished sorting through it all. I had similar thoughts when I started my decluttering journey. In fact, this is what every person who has a clutter problem thinks when they first begin their decluttering journey.

You can take a break and sit down to rest for a while, but don't give up. Just keep going through one item at a time. No matter how large your mountains of stuff become, you're still dealing with a finite amount of things. It may take you a long time to go through them, and that is totally fine, but there will definitely come a day when you'll cross the finish line as you decide what to do with your last item of clutter.

There is no specific timeline for how long it should take you to declutter. Every person requires a different amount of time based on the number of possessions they have and how good they are at deciding what to do with their belongings. The good news is that the more frequently you declutter, the better you get at executing the process.

Even though there is no one-size-fits-all timeline for how long it should take a person to declutter, you need to set a deadline for it; otherwise, you'll fall into the nasty tentacles of procrastination and delays. The deadline needs to be realistic. Thinking you can declutter your entire home in a day or two is downright unrealistic, especially if your clutter problem is very serious.

It is better to set aside a certain amount of time every day to devote to decluttering. How long this declutter routine should last depends on how much time you have at hand and the kind of responsibilities you're dealing with. You can try a decluttering marathon for a day or two for a smaller space. Some people have managed to declutter their entire home in a week or two, doing nothing but decluttering all day, every day. This doesn't work for everyone and probably can't even realistically fit into most people's schedules. You need to decide what kind of time you are willing to invest in this and get started. Set a deadline that puts some pressure on you but isn't impossible to achieve.

Exercise 8.4

Date:_____

Schedule decluttering sessions on your calendar and stick to the time you assign to them. Also, set a deadline for finishing the decluttering process for each area and for your entire home.

The Next Step: Organizing

Once you have finished decluttering, it's so much easier (and rather delightful) to organize the things you're left with. We'll discuss various organizing strategies in Part IV of the book. For now, I just want you to start getting in the habit of grouping items of a similar nature together. For instance, all of your tank tops can be held in one place, all your pens and writing tools can be stored in a specific drawer, etc. However, you want to finish the decluttering process first and then move on to organizing what you are left with. Trying to group both of these together is a recipe for disaster. You'll feel confused and overwhelmed as you haven't sorted out quite well what you want to keep with you. It's no wonder the "how" of storing them isn't very clear either.

Once you have things organized, you'll have to maintain a basic tidying schedule to keep them that way.

Maintaining a Basic Cleaning Schedule While You Are Going Through the Decluttering Process

I strongly recommend that you first finish the entire decluttering process and then form a proper routine for cleaning and tidying regularly. Cleaning and tidying take up very little time when we are surrounded only by the objects we love and enjoy having with us.

However, there are two things you must continue doing even when you are going through the decluttering process: laundry and dishes. To keep your house functional even while the decluttering process is going on, you have to regularly do the laundry and dishes. Do not go to bed with dirty dishes in the sink, or they'll never let you have a good night's sleep. Yes, I agree, there are some days when we are all way too tired to do the dishes, and tackling them the next morning makes more sense, but I caution you against making a habit out of this. It never feels good to be greeted by a huge load of dirty dishes in your kitchen first thing in the morning. You deserve to wake up to a clean, fresh kitchen.

Also, as soon as a load of dishes has been washed, try to put them away as quickly as possible. I was personally really bad at this. In fact, I was accustomed to pulling dishes out of the dishwasher immediately before use and putting them back in the dishwasher after use. But this really doesn't feel good. You deserve a beautiful kitchen where all your dishes are stacked properly and aesthetically. It's a delight to use items from such a kitchen!

The same concept applies to clothes. If your home generates a lot of laundry, then you may want to run a fresh load every day. Do it first thing in the morning or as soon as you can get to it. Make sure you aren't getting the clothes out of the washer and dryer only to leave them crumpled. Gather your determination to fold and put them away immediately. This does take discipline, and the five-second rule we discussed earlier in the book is an excellent tool for overcoming procrastination.

The idea behind staying on top of your laundry and dishes is that your house should remain functional even during marathon decluttering sessions. As long as you and your family have clean clothes to wear and food to eat, you are doing well. It's only a matter of time until your home comes into order, and you'll love spending every possible minute in it.

Exercise 8.5

Date:_____

If you have a pile of laundry laying around, take care of it. Wash the dirty dishes that are in your sink. Do these right now!

Chapter 9

How to Stay Motivated While Decluttering and Using Decluttering Checklists

"If you're not using the stuff in your home, get rid of it. You're not going to start using it more by shoving it in a closet somewhere."

— Joshua Becker (Hage, 2021)

Decluttering your home can be an extremely overwhelming project. You may feel like you're trapped inside a never-ending cave with not even a remote glimmer of light in sight. As I said in the previous chapter, as long as you're briefly pausing to rest only to resume the task at hand, you are doing well. No matter how large your mountain of stuff is, one day, you'll get to the very last item.

At the same time, I understand how hard it is to stay motivated while decluttering. There have been so many times when I wanted to throw in the towel and give up the project altogether. Maybe I was just meant to live a messy life, surrounded by mountains of clutter! But I am glad I didn't give up, and you'll be, too, once you reach the end of your decluttering project. No matter how long the journey may take, you're going to get there. You'll see and experience considerable improvement in your clutter situation as you consistently keep moving forward.

Take Before and After Pictures

One of the best ways to keep track of your progress is to take before and after pictures. Before tackling your clutter, take a picture of the space exactly as it is. Many people cringe at the idea of doing this, almost as if they can deny the reality of the situation if they can prevent it from being captured in a photograph.

Something very interesting happens when you take pictures: you can suddenly look at things from a different perspective. It's one thing to be living surrounded by all that clutter and another to look at it like another person does. Pictures are excellent for providing that third-person perspective. Pictures also compel you to observe many details you may otherwise miss while living in that space.

The idea of a space being photographed compels us to adhere to a much higher standard of neatness and tidiness. It is almost like we subconsciously start thinking that we aren't the only ones witnessing our space; through a photograph, anyone can. This makes us a lot more cautious about how we present it.

I recommend you start out by taking a picture of your space exactly as it is, and then as you organize and put things together, take more pictures. This will give you a visual representation of your work, and trust me, you will be enormously proud of yourself eventually.

If ever you feel you have gone back to living in clutterville, you can simply look at these pictures and remind yourself that if you did it once, you can do it again. However, once you have conquered your clutter for good, you will never go back to square one again. Yes, it may seem temporarily that you have gone back to being your old self, living the way you used to, but you will be able to fix the situation quickly. These photographs will serve as strong motivators to remind you of what you have achieved once. If you did it once, you can do it even better the next time.

Exercise 9.1

Date:_____

Take a "before" picture prior to beginning the decluttering process. As you start organizing and putting things together, take more pictures. You can print these pictures or store them in a digital file. Keeping the pictures side-by-side in a collage will help you stay mindful of how far you have come in your journey.

Even after you have completed the decluttering process, I strongly recommend that you regularly take pictures of your space to analyze how you can improve things. Pictures will help you see things you may not otherwise notice while living in that space.

Make it Fun

You are not alone if you're thinking right now that the words "decluttering" and "fun" don't go together. I was the same way. I hated every minute of decluttering! I realized the constant chatter inside my head that kept telling me how I wasn't good enough made things a lot worse for me. I started listening to my favorite music during decluttering sessions to keep my mind engaged in something else. I prefer and would recommend calming instrumental music. This way, you can still ask yourself questions about whether you want to keep or not keep something while allowing yourself to be soothed by the music.

Once you get better at assessing what to do with each item, you can even start doing it on autopilot. Over time, you build the mental muscle memory for it, and you can make the right decisions without having to spend too much time thinking about it. At that point, you can also start listening to things like podcasts, audiobooks, etc. You can very easily double-up your decluttering time as a learning hour.

Exercise 9.2

Date:_____

Play some beautiful instrumental music while decluttering.

A Word of Caution...

One thing I'd caution you not to do is declutter while someone else is around, unless maybe they're helping you out. It is best to declutter alone. If you invite another person to participate in the decluttering process, it may be hard to make the right decisions, as this person may unwittingly influence you. You may hear things like, "You might need it later," "It doesn't look too bad on you," or "I think it looks good on you." It could become difficult for you to figure out how you truly feel about something with this influence. Even worse, once you decide to discard or donate certain items, that person may want to take those items, even if they aren't actually useful to them. If they live in the same household as you, the clutter will continue to remain stuck inside your home, even if it is transferred to their area of the house.

Yes, you can help out a family member if they need your assistance with their own decluttering. In that case, you can teach them to ask the same questions I have taught you to assess what to do with each item. However, I would caution you to keep your decluttering projects confined to your personal territory. Don't try decluttering other family members' items without their permission, no matter how badly their clutter is bothering you. It is possible that what you view as clutter is a collection of priceless possessions for them. You can only inspire others through your example; you can't impose your will or your standards upon anyone.

I know this is tough for a perfectionist like you. You want to declutter every nook and cranny of your house, and it bothers you if even a corner is left as it is. But this is another important instance in which you must give up your perfectionism.

Keeping your relationships harmonious is just as important as living in a neat and tidy home, if not more so. Your family members may or may not be inspired by your example, but you must respect their choices and individuality in every way. You can't force them to adopt a different way of life just because you have. It's better to just be there for them and let them come to you for assistance if and when they want to.

Your example may rub off them and inspire them to also declutter their belongings. For now, you must stick to your area of the house. (If you have small children living with you, that could be an exception. In that case, you can take the liberty to declutter and organize their spaces, too. However, if your children are old enough to have their own likes and dislikes, it would be best to involve them.) As I mentioned in Book 1, it is a wonderful practice to start teaching kids how to stay neat and tidy from a young age. You can also organize fun decluttering and cleaning projects and get the entire family involved (if everyone is on board with it, of course).

If you live alone, obviously, you are free to do whatever you like!

Using Decluttering Checklists

Decluttering checklists always come in handy, but they can be particularly helpful when you feel unmotivated. So if you are not sure which items you should discard, refer to this list to see which ones resonate with you, and get rid of those items. Of course, this could mean discarding the item if it is absolutely not useful anymore or giving it to someone else if they can make better use of it. You can also add them to the command-Z box. However, keep in mind that a lot of these items are better tossed away than stored for later.

In the Closet

- Too many clothes hangers that you never use or need
- Tattered clothes

- Old t-shirts with holes
- Old, worn-out sneakers
- Pieces of jewelry you don't like wearing and that don't have much monetary value
- Socks without their match or with holes
- Anything that no longer fits you and that you don't intend to get altered
- Pantyhose with tears and holes
- Ill-fitting shoes

Linen and Home Decor

- Rugs or any decor item you don't use
- Extra pillows that occupy space in your house but never get used
- Bed linen with holes or significant signs of wear
- Candles that are never lit and also don't serve any aesthetic purpose
- Knick-knacks that are never displayed and usually just gather dust
- Cleaning rags that are too dirty to be washed
- Towels with holes or other significant signs of wear

In the Kitchen

- Any food item that has expired
- Plastic cutlery saved from food deliveries that you won't realistically ever be using
- Plastic containers with missing lids
- Knives that are too blunt to be of any use
- Vacuum flasks that no longer keep beverages hot or cold

- Cookie cutters and other baking tools that never get used
- Bent cake pans and baking trays
- Broken utensils

In the Bathroom

- Expired makeup
- Toiletries that are never used
- Hairstyling tools that don't work anymore
- Stained or worn-out shower curtains
- Expired medicine
- Dried-up nail polish
- Expired sunscreen and other grooming products
- Makeup that has never been used and likely never going to be used
- Empty bottles and containers of used-up products
- Melted soap
- Unused cologne and perfume

In the Bedroom and Living Room

- Items tucked under the bed that are never actually used
- Melted candles that aren't usable anymore
- Broken furniture that can't be fixed
- Dying plants
- Wilted flowers
- Broken decor pieces

Paper Clutter

- Old bills and paychecks that are never going to be needed (especially if you have them in digital format, anyway)
- Old newspaper
- Outdated calendars
- Notebooks you don't use and that just aren't aesthetically pleasing enough
- Expired coupons
- Used-up planners
- Ticket stubs
- Take-out menus (you can find the most up-to-date ones with the click of a button)
- Grocery store newsletters
- Old magazines you haven't flipped through in ages
- Books you are never going to read or read again

Technology and Entertainment

- Mobile phones/laptops that don't work
- Earphones you never use
- Old CDs and VHS tapes, especially if you don't have a player for them
- Toys that no one plays with
- Puzzles or other games with missing pieces
- Cords that aren't compatible with any of your current devices
- Chargers that no longer work
- Old screen protectors and phone covers
- Stuffed animals that neither you nor family members like having around
- Old TVs that don't function or are never used
- Video games and/or board games that no one really plays with

Miscellaneous

- Projects left in an unfinished state
- Old, dried-out paint
- Old product boxes with the contents used up
- Broken flower pots
- Anything that doesn't work anymore (either get it fixed or get rid of it!)
- Expired cleaning supplies
- Keychains you don't use
- Refrigerator magnets that don't make you happy but make your refrigerator look cluttered
- Duplicate tape measures
- Old party supplies
- Tools and machinery that are rusting
- Seasonal holiday decor that is never actually used

What to Do with Sentimental Items

If you've read the first book, you already know what I have to say on this subject. I know parting with sentimental items can be extremely tough. We feel guilty classifying something that has been lovingly given or passed on to us as clutter. However, the truth is that if something is never used or truly valued, it is clutter. This doesn't diminish the value or importance of the person who has given the item to us. We must learn to separate our feelings for the person from our feelings for the item we've received from that person. They are not one and the same thing; the two must never be confused together.

In Book 1, I suggested that you give the item away to someone who would get better use out of it. If the idea of giving the item away still doesn't appeal to you, then I have a few more suggestions for you. There are two things you can do:

- Take a picture, and then give the item away. This way, you'll always have the memory of the item with you, and you can recall all the wonderful emotions you feel towards the person by looking at the picture of their gift to you.
- Try to put the item to alternative uses. For instance, a coffee mug you don't like drinking coffee out of can serve as a stationary holder on your work table. Similarly, a dress you aren't ever going to wear can become a cushion cover (if you know how to sew or can take it to a seamstress). Every item can be put to some kind of alternative use; think creatively and you'll be able to come up with something.

Exercise 9.3

Date:_____

Create a list of all the sentimental items that don't make you happy but are difficult to part with. Once you have the list ready, write down 1-3 alternative uses to which you can put each item.

Part Four

Mastering the Art of Organizing and Living Clutter-Free

Chapter 10
How to Organize Your Home and Your Life

"For every minute spent organizing, an hour is earned."

— Benjamin Franklin (Order Your Life, 2018)

The next most important task after decluttering is organizing. Through organizing, you want to bring a sense of order and functionality to your space. Before you begin organizing your belongings, create a vision for how you would like to approach your space.

Here are some questions to think about before you start organizing:

- How can you make the best use of the space available to you? Are you storing items that fit appropriately in the space available to you, or do you have smaller items taking up lots of space when that space can be used to store bigger items?

- What are the ways in which you can maximize space? For instance, you can use closet dividers, shelf organizers, and hanging organizers to maximize the space in your closet.

Place Your Most Frequently Used Items in an Accessible Location

The most important thing to remember with organizing is that you want to place your most frequently used items in the front, and those items you don't reach out for often at an intuitive location. You want to be able to find the latter when you need it, but you don't need to have it at an easy-to-reach location. For instance, in my closets and cupboards, I place the items I reach out for daily or very frequently at eye level. I reserve the top and bottom shelves for items I don't use as frequently. I still do my best to keep items of a similar type grouped together. This way, I know exactly where I can find an item when I am looking for it.

Important Organizational Methods and Techniques

There are several very simple tricks and methods that you can use to organize your space. I'm going to share some of my most favorite methods here.

Labeling

This is one of the most effective ways of distinguishing items from each other. You can use different types of labels. For instance, I love using chalkboard-type label stickers in my pantry. You can erase and rewrite these types of labels as they come with chalk or a chalk-style pen. But to be very honest, they don't erase that well. It's best to write just once and store your desired item in the container labeled for it. If you must erase the writing, it would be a good idea to use some glass cleaning spray and wipe off the writing with a microfiber cloth.

I also strongly recommend getting a label maker. They aren't that expensive and can be easily bought online. I've had mine for a very long time, and it has turned out to be a worthy investment. As much as I love labeling things, I would caution you against over-labeling, or your home will start resembling a meticulous instruction manual!

It is better to do the labeling in more subtle ways:

- **Labeling in hidden places:** You can place the labels in areas that aren't directly visible to the eye. For instance, inside a cabinet, you can place the labels on the top surface of the shelf. Similarly, you can place the label under the box or in any other area where you will have to make a slight effort to find the label, but it shouldn't be too much of a strain.
- **Buy organizers with built-in slots for labels:** Labels look a lot more natural inside the built-in labeling slots of organizers.
- **Buy pre-labeled organizers:** This is undoubtedly the most elegant option. You can buy containers for specific purposes that have been pre-labeled, for instance, a beautiful jar with "sugar" written on it or a cookie jar that has cookies drawn all over it.

Color Coding

This is another excellent method for organizing different items categorically. You can buy bins in different colors and use each color to store items belonging to a specific category. For instance, I store all my heat-styling tools in a blue bin, but my hair products go inside a purple bin. Having separate colors for these different categories helps me easily find the item I am looking for.

Color coding is also excellent for helping children stay organized. You can assign different colored storage containers to each child. Even very small children will be able to keep their items organized when they know in which color container all their items should go into.

Using Transparent Organizers

Using transparent organizers is excellent for keeping items visible and, hence, easily accessible. You get to "label" the items without using an actual label. This method works really well for organizing spaces where you'd regularly be changing labels. For instance, you can get clear containers for organizing different items in your refrigerator.

Stack Items Vertically Instead of Horizontally

This is something I learned from Marie Kondo. Marie advises you to keep folded items vertically stacked together instead of horizontally on top of one another. This prevents the disaster that happens when items are stacked horizontally on top of one another: you try pulling one item out, and everything else falls out of place, as well. When items are vertically stacked together inside a bin or drawer, there isn't any possibility of the other items falling apart every time you pull one item out.

Marie Kondo recommends a very specific method of folding which you can easily learn from her YouTube videos. It's definitely worth learning her folding techniques for various clothing items.

Use Bins and Baskets Generously

I seriously feel that I can never have too many organizers. No matter how many organizers I buy, I end up using all of them. You could say I'm addicted to organizers! While there are organizers available for every possible purpose from neatly storing your cleaning supplies to organizing your tech gadgets, I suggest you start with the very basics. Your first goal should be to acquire plastic boxes, bins, and baskets in various colors. Just make sure the colors you place together in any space go harmoniously together. You may even want to adopt a monochrome color theme for certain areas, using organizational supplies in just one color.

The easiest way to make any space look put-together is to place items belonging to a specific category inside a bin or basket. This also makes cleaning closets and cupboard surfaces a breeze because you can very easily pull everything out as all things will be stored in their respective baskets. This is one of my favorite hacks for reducing cleaning time.

Lisa Hedberg

Exercise 10.1

Date:_____

Now, it's time to determine what kind of organizational supplies you should shop for. If you don't have the budget for it right now, you can use whatever boxes and cartons you have lying around the house. To make such boxes more aesthetically pleasing, you can cover them with colorful craft paper. No matter your budget, there is no excuse for not putting in the effort to get organized. If you don't have ample money to buy new supplies for organizing, you can use your creativity to make your own. There are plenty of tutorials online that can instruct you on how to do it.

If you can spare money on new organizers, there's nothing like it. You can get very cheap plastic organizers at discount stores. Most of them look decent and work perfectly well. Organizers meant for specific purposes can be quite expensive; I suggest you save those for last. Start by purchasing bins, boxes, and baskets. These are going to be the most versatile organizers you'll end up using everywhere in your house.

Organizational Tools and Supplies Checklist

Think about one space at a time and write down the number of each item you'll need. Of course, tools like a label maker need to be bought only once, but the tape needed for it may have to be replenished from time to time. As for supplies like baskets, bins, and boxes, you'll need them according to the space you are trying to organize.

I suggest you make photocopies of the checklist below so that you can use a separate sheet for each space you are working on. (Don't forget to download the free printable exercises and checklists; the link is at the front of this book!) Mark a ✓ next to the item that you intend to buy or that you already own. In the blank space under the item name, you can write down the number of each item you'll need. This way, you'll have all the supplies and tools at hand when working on organizing a particular space.

Tools

- Label stickers

Number: ___

- CD marker pens for writing on label stickers

Number: ___

- Chalkboard stickers

Number: ___

- Chalkboard pencil for writing on blackboard stickers

Number: 1

- Label maker

Number: 1

- Label maker tape

Number: ___

- Scissors

Number: 1 pair

Supplies

Along with the total number of items you need, I would also recommend writing down the color(s) and size(s) in which you intend to get them. If you aren't sure what each of these items is, you can look them up online. As I said earlier, pick only what suits you.

- Baskets

Number: ___ Colors: _____

- Bins

Number: ___ Colors: _____

- Boxes

Number: ___ Colors: _____

- Clear baskets

Number: ___ Colors: _____

- Clear bins

Number: ___ Colors: _____

- Clear boxes

Number: ___ Colors: _____

- Drawer dividers

Number: ___ Colors: _____

- Stackable drawers

Number: ___ Colors: _____

- Sliding basket drawers

Number: ___ Colors: _____

- Rack organizers

Number: ___ Colors: _____

- Pots and pans organizer

Number: ___ Colors: _____

- Cord organizer

Number: ___ Colors: _____

- Under sink organizer

Number: ___ Colors: _____

- Rotating turntable organizer

Number: ___ Colors: _____

- Shoe organizer

Number: ___ Colors: _____

- Under bed organizer

Number: ___ Colors: _____

- Hanging clothes organizers

Number: ___ Colors: _____

- Hangers

Number: ___ Colors: _____

- Storage cart

Number: ___ Colors: _____

- Underwear organizer

Number: ___ Colors: _____

- Spice rack organizer

Number: ___ Colors: _____

- Spice drawer organizer

Decluttering Workbook

Number: ___ Colors: _____

- Pre-labelled boxes/bins/baskets

Number: ___ Colors: _____

- Wall-mounted broom holder

Number: ___ Colors: _____

- Paper letter tray organizer

Number: ___ Colors: _____

- File holders/desk organizers

Number: ___ Colors: _____

- Bookends

Number: ___ Colors: _____

- Makeup organizer

Number: ___ Colors: _____

- Electronics organizer

Number: ___ Colors: _____

- Shower caddy

Number: ___ Colors: _____

Tips for Organizing Your Closet

As I mentioned at the beginning of the chapter, first, you have to look at the space available to you, then think about the different ways in which you can maximize the space. Here are some of my favorite tips for making your closet look beautiful and organized:

- Store out-of-season clothes out of sight in large boxes or bins. You can buy aesthetically pleasing clothes bins. Large hat boxes and gift boxes are also excellent options for storing out-of-season items away from sight.
- If possible, use the same type and color of hangers for your entire closet. For instance, if you use wooden hangers in white, stick with that. If you use beige velvet hangers, use the same for all your clothing items.
- Hang items like shirts, blouses, skirts, dresses, jackets, and trousers.
- T-shirts and workout clothes can be folded and stacked vertically inside organizer bins placed on the shelves of your closet.
- Group items of a similar type together. For instance, dresses can be one group, jackets can be another, etc.
- Create color blocks within each item category. To look visually pleasing, you should arrange clothes from light to dark.
- To maximize the shelving area, use stackable shelves. This way, you can easily take out whatever you need while making the best use of your space.

Exercise 10.2

Date:_____

Create a list of organizational supplies you need for organizing your closet area.

Lisa Hedberg

Develop a mental image of what you would like your fully organized closet to look like. If you are artistically inclined, drawing a blueprint will help you gain further clarity. Use the space below to make a rough drawing of what the closet will look like after you have finished organizing it.

Paste before and after pictures of your closet area below.

Tips for Organizing Your Kitchen and Pantry Area

A beautifully organized kitchen and pantry area can turn cooking into a delightful experience. Here are some tips to make this area beautiful, functional, and organized:

- Use clear containers made specifically for refrigerators to organize your refrigerator shelves. These clear containers come in all kinds of shapes and sizes. You want to arrange them to fill the majority of the space in your refrigerator; then, you can just keep stocking items inside them according to your needs. You can use these containers for versatile storage needs: one week, you can store a sandwich in a container, and another week, it can be utilized for storing potatoes.
- Divide the pantry into different sections. For instance, you can have a section for breakfast cereals, another for dry beans, another one for baking goods, etc. The idea is to group items of a similar nature together to make everything easily accessible. Labeling the containers can be extremely helpful in the pantry area. I personally love using chalkboard stickers on these containers, and I also use pre-labeled jars for various items. My pro tip for keeping your pantry area looking beautiful is to use the same type of storage containers in the entire area. For instance, if you use glass jars, try to use the same size and type of glass jars in the entire pantry.
- Place frequently used cooking utensils at easily accessible locations. Items you don't often use, like

baking utensils and tools, can be stored in less easily accessible areas.
- Use pots and pans dividers to keep them functionally organized.
- Use drawer dividers to neatly store all your cutlery and miscellaneous kitchen tools.
- Use plate holders to vertically stack your plates inside kitchen cabinets.
- Store items of a similar type together. For instance, bowls of the same size and color should be stacked together; the same idea applies to plates and other items.
- You can organize your spices either inside a drawer or on a spice rack. The spice rack can be stored inside a cabinet. I personally like to keep my countertops uncluttered and bare. This makes cleaning easy; plus, it gives me a sense of calm when I can walk inside my kitchen every morning to see it isn't looking "too busy."

Exercise 10.3

Date:_____

Create a list of organizational supplies you need for organizing your kitchen and pantry area.

Decluttering Workbook

Develop a mental image of what you would like the fully organized kitchen/pantry area to look like. If you are artistically inclined, drawing a blueprint will help you gain further clarity. Use the space below to make a rough drawing of what the kitchen will look like after you have finished organizing the area.

Paste before and after pictures of your kitchen and pantry area below.

Tips for Organizing Your Bathroom Area

We all love a beautiful bathroom that looks fit for Cleopatra! Yet, such a bathroom eludes most people. I've got some great ideas to make your bathrooms look and feel luxurious on any budget.

- Divide the items you use in the bathroom into different categories and assign a "home" for each category.
- Decide where the "home" for each item category should be, for instance, under the sink, in the shower area, inside the medicine cabinet, in the linen closet, etc.
- Use a shower caddy to store all your bath products.
- To make your bathroom more aesthetically pleasing, remove all packaging containers. Decant all items into clear plastic/glass or ceramic containers. If you are sharing the bathroom with others, then each person can have their own caddy with their own set of decanted products stored in clear containers; if you feel that would cause confusion, you can buy pre-packaged containers. This is the best tip for making any bathroom look instantly luxurious. Obviously, I do not recommend using glass containers in the bathroom if you have children around.
- Use the area under the sink to store frequently used items. But as I said in Book 1, be careful not to store anything there that can be impacted by moisture, like an electric shaver or any battery-operated device. Keep everything neatly categorized by storing

different types of items in color-coded bins/baskets/boxes.
- You can store items with their original packaging in closets and cabinets. This way, you can still access them easily, but the packaging isn't displayed inside the bathroom like an eyesore.
- Use the linen closet to store your sheets and towels. Again, use bins to store everything vertically.

Exercise 10.4

Date:_____

Create a list of organizational supplies you need for organizing your bathroom area.

Develop a mental image of what you would like the fully organized bathroom to look like. If you are artistically inclined, drawing a blueprint will help you gain further clarity. Use the space below to make a rough drawing of what your bathroom will look like after you have finished organizing it.

Paste before and after pictures of your bathroom area below.

Tips for Organizing Your Study/Home Office

A clean desk with minimum items on display induces a sense of calm and enables you to be at your creative best. Having a functionally organized and aesthetically pleasing home office becomes all the more essential if you are someone who, like me, works from home.

- Use metal bookends to keep books vertically stacked on shelves and other areas you like to display them. This way, you can pull out one book and shift the bookend a little so that the books still remain perfectly vertically stacked.
- Use filing cabinets or file storage boxes for storing all your files.
- Desk organizers can come in handy for keeping stationery and other such items beautifully displayed and easily accessible.
- Buy a document organizer and folders for storing all your important paperwork.
- Maximize drawer space by using drawer dividers. You can use adjustable drawer dividers that easily allow you to modify the layout whenever needed.

Exercise 10.5

Date:_____

Create a list of organizational supplies you need for organizing your study/home office area.

. . .

Develop a mental image of what you would like the fully organized study/office area to look like. If you are artistically inclined, drawing a blueprint will help you gain further clarity. Use the space below to make a rough drawing of what the area will look like after you have finished organizing it.

Paste before and after pictures of your study/home office area below.

Tips for Organizing Your Cleaning Supplies Aesthetically

While cleaning supplies play an essential role in helping us maintain a clean and tidy space, it can be difficult to keep them organized in a way that looks aesthetically pleasing. Let's explore some options for storing cleaning supplies in a more aesthetically pleasing manner.

- Store them behind closed doors whenever possible. This could mean making maximum use of the area under the sink or an extra storage cabinet.
- Prepare a cleaning caddy by placing all the cleaning supplies you need daily in the caddy. You can pull out this caddy and take it with you every day when you are ready to clean. You can buy a caddy with a handle for this purpose.
- Use wall-mounted broom organizers in storage closets to hang all your brooms and mops.
- Use cabinet door-mounted organizers for storing your kitchen and bathroom cleaning supplies.
- You can also consider decanting cleaning products into clear plastic containers or spray bottles if the labels and packaging boxes bother you too much.
- Keep all your cleaning supplies neatly organized in different categories. Use boxes/bins/baskets wherever necessary.

Lisa Hedberg

Exercise 10.6

Date:_____

Create a list of organizational supplies you need for organizing your cleaning supplies.

Develop a mental image of what you would like the fully organized cleaning supplies area to look like. If you are artistically inclined, drawing a blueprint will help you gain further clarity. Use the space below to make a rough drawing of what the area will look like after you have finished organizing it.

Paste before and after pictures of your cleaning supplies storage area below.

Chapter 11
Routines and Checklists

"With consistency and reps and routine you're going to achieve your goals and get where you want to be."

— Mandy Rose ("Routine Quotes," n.d.)

The best way to keep your house beautiful is by maintaining a regular routine of cleaning and tidying. You should have lists categorizing all the important tasks that need to be performed regularly. Maintaining lists of things that need to be done around the house is essential if you want to live in an aesthetically pleasing and highly functional home.

Don't Be a Perfectionist

I really want you to ditch your perfectionism when it comes to performing housework. You are never going to be able to do everything perfectly. As long as you are doing at least the basics regularly, you are doing well.

Also, you must keep your standards flexible for those times when your situation changes. For instance, having company over, the arrival of new babies, long working hours, stressful life events, etc. are all good reasons to allow your regular routine to be interrupted. During such times, you have to establish and define your priorities. Nothing matters more than the health, safety, and comfort of the people living in your home. In such times, clutter, organization, entertainment, and appearances can be allowed to take a backseat. You can always return back to your original schedule as soon as you start feeling ready for it. But don't be too hard on yourself. As I said earlier, the goal isn't to live in an uncluttered, beautiful home; your goal is to live a happy, peaceful, and beautiful life in a harmonious house that reflects your inner persona.

Stick to a minimal, workable routine when maintaining your ideal routine seems too hard to do. You are doing well if you and your family have healthy meals to eat, clean dishes to eat food from, and fresh clothes to wear. It is also a good idea to at least keep the bedroom vacuumed, dusted, and well-aired. Bedding should also be changed frequently to maintain hygiene.

Routines and Checklists

In this section, I will share with you some sample routines. Feel free to modify these to suit your individual needs, as some things may be relevant to you while others may not.

I strongly recommend that you photocopy or print these routines. Keep them handy to stay on top of your schedule and mark each item after you have completed it daily. You can use an online resource or an app on your phone to keep track of the tasks you have accomplished. You can also place your routines in a file with each routine stored securely in its own waterproof document sleeve. Use a dry erase marker to checkmark each item once the task has been completed. At the end of the day, you can wipe the waterproof sheet with a microfiber cloth. Use glass cleaning spray to remove any marker stains more neatly.

Daily Routine

- Make beds
- Place soiled clothes in laundry hamper and hang/fold all other clothes
- Run a fresh load of laundry. This can be either a daily task or a weekly one, depending upon the size of your household. Just stay on top of your laundry!
- Wipe phones with a microfiber cloth
- Clean computer surfaces and keyboards
- Change the water for flowers, remove wilted petals, and prune the ends
- Water the plants
- Clean all sinks at least once after use (including traps and drains)
- Clean the bathtub area after taking a shower/bath (including traps and drains)
- Clean bathroom counters and toilets
- Check/refill essential supplies in the bathroom (like soap, toilet paper, shampoo, conditioner, toothpaste, etc.)
- Put out fresh kitchen towels and place the used ones in the laundry hamper

- Prepare food and clean up afterward
- Wipe kitchen countertops after each use
- Wipe the stove area
- Run a load of dirty dishes in the dishwasher
- Put clean and dried dishes away
- Clean the floors in frequently used areas like the kitchen, living room, and main entryway
- Refill humidifiers and vaporizers (also, clean them if needed)
- Shopping for essentials and groceries (whenever necessary)
- Take out the trash and place fresh garbage bags in the trash containers
- Tidy for 20 minutes (place items back in their "home" + discard items that are no longer needed)

Weekly Routine

You can assign each major task to a specific day of the week. Dividing the list in this manner will help you accomplish multiple tasks without feeling overwhelmed. Once you have established a day for each major task of the week, it would be a good idea to stick to it long-term. Over time, you'll get accustomed to associating that specific day of the week with the task you have to perform.

What if you miss out on completing the task on the day assigned to it? In that case, simply perform the missed task along with the task listed for the next day.

Here is a list suggesting how you can use different days of the week to accomplish various tasks:

- Monday – Washing and ironing

- Tuesday – Miscellaneous odd jobs
- Wednesday – Minor housecleaning
- Thursday – Shopping for groceries and essentials
- Friday – Sorting through paper clutter; cleaning out handbags
- Saturday – Decluttering + organizing + major house cleaning
- Sunday – Holiday

Weekly Tasks Checklist

Here is a list of house cleaning chores you may want to perform weekly. Again, use your discretion to add or remove items from the list. You can assign the tasks to different days of the week to suit your personal schedule and needs.

- Change bed linens once or twice every week
- Wash all washable floors
- Vacuum rugs, carpeted surfaces, lampshades, and upholstered furniture
- Vacuum faux flowers and other home decor items
- Replace wilted flowers with fresh ones
- Dust all surfaces that require dusting, including light fixtures, picture frames, and artwork
- Wipe doors and doorknobs
- Wipe all closet and cabinet doors
- Dust windows and wipe the surface of windows
- Wipe all mirrors
- Deep clean the bathroom (including all areas like sink, bathtub, toilet, wall tiles, toothbrush holders, cabinet exteriors and shelves, floor, mirror, etc.)
- Deep clean the kitchen (remove unwanted/wipe items from the refrigerator, wipe refrigerator

surfaces, wipe the exterior of ovens/microwaves, clean sinks, tabletops, countertops, scrub floors)
- Clean humidifiers and air conditioner filters (if needed)
- Wash all combs and hairbrushes
- Take clothes to the dry cleaners

Monthly/Quarterly/Seasonal Checklist

Here is a checklist for recommended tasks that should be performed monthly or quarterly. Some of the tasks need to be performed each season.

- Launder mattress covers and pillow covers (the innermost pillowcase, inside which the actual pillow rests, not the case that matches your bedsheets) (monthly)
- Deep clean the entryway (monthly)
- Clean under heavy furniture and appliances (quarterly)
- Declutter and organize the garden area (quarterly or whenever needed)
- Dust blinds and all hard-to-reach areas that collect dust (monthly)
- Deep clean the oven and microwave (depending upon usage, you can either have this as a monthly task or a quarterly task)
- Rotate all mattresses (quarterly)
- Clean all fans (quarterly)
- Wax floors (quarterly or whenever needed)
- Wax wooden surfaces (quarterly or whenever needed)

- Declutter and reorganize all frequently used cabinets, drawers, and closets (monthly or quarterly)
- Give away unused/unworn items (monthly)
- Clean the garage (quarterly)

Annual/Semiannual Checklist

This is a list of tasks that should be performed annually or semiannually; use your discretion to decide what works best for you. Of course, some of these items may not apply to you, so feel free to edit the list to suit your needs and living situation.

- Get blankets, comforters, and quilts dry-cleaned. You can also wash them if the manufacturer's instructions prescribe that.
- Clean and store out-of-season clothes away from sight; replace with seasonal clothing (every spring and fall season)
- Polish and clean all silverware
- Clean and polish all precious jewelry items
- Deep clean all walls, floors, and ceilings
- Clean the basement area
- Vacuum books
- Shampoo upholstery and rugs
- Empty and deep clean all drawers, closets, and cabinets
- Wash blinds and windows
- Wash or dry-clean curtains and draperies
- Organize and declutter gadgets
- Donate or discard gadgets and tools that are no longer needed

Checklist for Those Days When You Can't Do the Full Routine

Use this checklist whenever you are lacking the time, energy, or willpower needed to perform your regular routine.

- Make the bed (change bed linen at least once a week)
- Wash dirty dishes
- Prepare food you can cook quickly or use pre-packaged meals
- Restock essential pantry items
- Wipe kitchen countertops
- Scrub the kitchen sink
- Clean the toilet
- Wipe bathroom countertop
- Dust and vacuum only those areas where you and other family members spend the maximum amount of their time
- Run a fresh load of laundry
- Put things back in place after each use

For Those Times When You are Feeling Overwhelmed…

We all go through those times when things feel way too overwhelming. During such times, it's worth considering outsourcing some of the housekeeping work. If you can fit it into your budget, hiring cleaning help is a good idea. You can call a cleaning service company in your local area and have a maid come in for a day (or half a day) to help you out with the weekly cleaning tasks.

The checklists will come in really handy when you assign tasks to someone else. Hired cleaners will know exactly what is expected of them, which will help you maintain the cleanliness and tidiness of your space.

You can also consider hiring someone to help do the annual/semi-annual deep cleaning tasks. To save time on grocery shopping, you can start ordering groceries online. If you are very particular about using the freshest produce, then you can also foster an agreement with a local farm to deliver fresh produce once every week. Try to produce less laundry, and if you already have a large pile of it, then consider sending it out to a laundry service company.

When the situation is very serious (like during a major illness, childbirth, or death in the family), speak up and ask for the help of close friends and family. Most of the time, our loved ones are eager to help us; they just don't know how to do it. Tell them honestly how you would like them to help you, and this can significantly ease your burden.

Exercise 11.1

Date:_____

Photocopy/print the above checklists or refer to the free printable checklists; the link is at the front of this book. You can also create your own using the checklists in this chapter as an inspiration. Also, don't forget to download the 7 Tips to Declutter Your Life free eBook for some additional decluttering hacks; the link is at the front of this book!

You can digitally track the completion of each task, or you can use a file to store your checklists. Place each checklist inside a waterproof, transparent document sleeve and mark each task with a dry erase pen after it has been completed. Erase the markings when you need to use the checklist again. Alternatively, you can use whiteboards to write down your checklists and mark your progress.

Chapter 12

Pro Tips on Living a Clutter-Free Life

> *"In the never-ending battle between order and chaos, clutter sides with chaos every time. Anything that you possess that does not add to your life or your happiness eventually becomes a burden."*
>
> — John Robbins (Hage, 2021)

The best strategy for tackling clutter is to simply prevent it from entering your life and your physical space. Easier said than done; I know! Learning to distinguish clutter from the items we truly love and value is an art in itself. But the good news is that you get better at it the more frequently you practice.

Questions to Ask Yourself Before Buying/Bringing in Any New Item

It does take a tremendous amount of self-reflection and self-awareness to prevent clutter from entering your home. To ease the process of identifying potential clutter before it enters your space, here is a checklist of questions you may want to ask yourself before buying or bringing in any new item.

- Do I really need this?
- Am I buying this because it serves a definite purpose for me, or am I feeling tempted to buy it because it's being offered at a discounted price?
- How many times do I intend to use it?
- Where will I store it? (You should be able to clearly visualize a "home" for each item that you add to your space.)
- What will happen to it when it is no longer useful to me?
- Is it truly worth the money I'm willing to spend on it?
- What's going to be its cost per wear/cost per use?
- Is there another item that better serves my needs and preferences?
- Am I buying this just because it's cheaper than the item I actually want?
- Would I really regret not buying it?
- Can I postpone buying it and take my time to decide whether or not this is something truly valuable to me?
- For how long do I see myself using this item?
- Are there any maintenance costs associated with keeping this item in a functional/useful condition?
- What is the total cost of this product if I add the maintenance cost to the initial cost of the product?
- Do I see myself taking good care of this item?
- Does it match my personality/taste/style?

Decluttering Workbook

Exercise 12.1

Date:_____

Create a copy of this checklist and keep it with you at all times, whether in paper form or in digital form. Before making any purchase, ask yourself these questions. You'll realize that a lot of items you feel tempted to buy are things you don't actually need.

Marketers understand the lure of discount prices. While we think we are saving money, most of the time, we are really just spending money on things that neither make us truly happy nor meet any specific need of ours.

Using this checklist will help you save time, money, and energy. You'll buy less, but you'll buy more of the things that truly add value to your life. You'll feel good about your ability as a decision-maker. Since you are judiciously assessing each potential purchase, you are less likely to make blunders in the form of accumulated clutter.

Buy High Quality Items that Last Longer

The allure of discount prices is unmistakable. We go to the store to buy one shirt but end up returning home with four t-shirts because we managed to get all four at the price of one! Sounds like a great deal. Isn't it? Not really! You have to start thinking about the *true* cost of an item based on how much it costs you per use/wear. If you are buying a $10 t-shirt that looks decent for only two wears, that's a splurge. On the other hand, an organic cotton shirt sold at $60 that will last you a couple of years is a steal because the cost per wear is much lower.

Another important thing to consider is how the item makes you feel when you are wearing/using it. A low-quality discount-store t-shirt is unlikely to make you feel like a million bucks, but a high-quality shirt made out of premium materials that lasts a long time gives you the feeling of being on top of the world.

Start investing in items that make you feel good and add real value to your life. Don't let discounts and price reductions tempt you, or you'll just keep accumulating more clutter. It's totally worth saving up and splurging more on items you truly value and like having. A purchase isn't really extravagant or unjustified if it significantly improves the quality of your life or how you feel about yourself.

Your goal should be to live in a house and work in a space surrounded only by those items you truly love. You deserve to live in such a home! It's very difficult to have a clutter problem when you follow the basic principle of buying only those things that truly add value to your life.

Exercise 12.2

Date:_____

Create a wishlist of items you truly want to buy. For a few moments, forget about the sticker price of each item. Just think about what you would buy if money wasn't a constraint. Identify a few items that are currently within your budget and create a strategy for buying them. (For instance, you may have to forgo buying several cheap items in order to spend money on one item you truly want.)

Before making the final purchase, use the checklist from the previous section to identify whether or not this item would be truly valuable to you.

Conclusion

Thank you for placing your trust in me! I really hope this book has been a life-changing experience for you. If you have steadily worked through the teachings of each chapter and diligently completed every single exercise listed in this book, I am sure you have strong results to show by now.

If you haven't yet gotten the results you are looking for, it's okay! Just go back to the first chapter and slowly work through the contents of this book, implementing just one thing at a time. Every person is different. Hence, the time required by each person to get the results they are looking for is also going to be different. As I said at the beginning of the book, the most important thing is to be loving and compassionate to yourself.

Also, don't forget that decluttering and organizing are processes that never end. No matter how many times you declutter a specific area, it may become cluttered again. This is especially true if you have a large family in which each family member has a different temperament.

Remember that no matter how bad the clutter looks, you will never go back to square one. When you had a serious clutter problem, you didn't have all the tools, tips, techniques, tricks, and methods that you now have. By applying what you have learned through this book in a systematic manner, you can quickly declutter and reorganize any space.

Decluttering and organizing must happen regularly. This is why I've added them to the routines checklists (which I hope you are using regularly). The journey is the goal; you've got to start loving and enjoying it. Look at decluttering and organizing as acts of love and gratitude towards the items that serve you.

Decluttering Your Kitchen in 5 Easy Steps

Cutting Edge Strategies to Declutter, Clean and Organize Your Kitchen Without the Stress

"Clutter is not just the stuff on your floor – it's anything that stands between you and the life you want to be living."

— *Peter Walsh*

Introduction

Your kitchen is the lung of your house. The rest of the house cannot breathe properly if the kitchen is cluttered and disorganized. Now, I am not suggesting that you should aim to have one of those picture-perfect kitchens from home decor magazines. Your kitchen is not a static space meant for aesthetic pleasure alone. It is a dynamic living space that performs one of the most essential functions of the human experience – the noble task of nourishing you and your family.

If you are like most people, then your kitchen is also a space where a lot of life happens. Maybe you help your kids out with their homework on the dining table, you make plans for the next day, and perhaps, in winters, your family hangs out a lot there since it is so comforting to breathe in the aroma of warm food cooking.

Even if all you ever do in this special space of your home is cook the occasional meal, your kitchen should be a pleasure to work in. It should motivate and inspire you (and your family) to cook healthy meals. When you are in a disorga-

Introduction

nized and cluttered kitchen, it is hard to find anything in time. You get frustrated, scurrying around to find one ingredient after another. This ends up doubling or even tripling your total cooking time. Next time when you are hungry, you feel petrified at the idea of going through the same process all over again. It feels a lot simpler and easier to just order take-out.

Sound like you?

You have my full empathy. I was exactly like you. I thought I hated cooking, but the truth was I just hated cooking in a chaotic kitchen. If you dread the idea of preparing another home-cooked meal, I would challenge you to revisit that assumption once you have decluttered and organized your kitchen.

I want you to have a kitchen that makes you feel nourished and inspired every time you step into it. It should be functional enough to reduce cooking time to the minimum. Trust me, it really doesn't take that long to prepare healthy, wholesome meals for yourself and your family when you know exactly where everything is in your kitchen.

Once you get rid of the excess, it also becomes easier to keep the kitchen looking neat and clean. In this book, I will share with you my very best strategies for decluttering and organizing the kitchen. I will also share with you a cleaning and tidying schedule that is simple and easy to follow.

At this point, it may seem impossible that you'll ever be able to transform your kitchen. But I can promise you that if you implement everything I am sharing in this book, then you WILL definitely get the results. My kitchen was so bad that I could not set foot in it without risking slipping on bottle

Introduction

openers, cereal boxes, or empty food cans that had been lying around for days. If I can do it, then so can you. I believe in you. All I am asking for is that you take the chance and trust me with this – by the time you're done with this book, your kitchen and how you feel about it will have transformed completely (provided you follow all the instructions and do the work!). I am giving you this guarantee – all you have to do is put into practice everything I am teaching you here.

You deserve a beautiful and organized kitchen that is a delight to be in! So let us get started without any further ado!

Chapter 1
Assessing and Planning

"By failing to prepare, you are preparing to fail."

— *Benjamin Franklin (Brainy Quote, n.d.)*

It doesn't matter whether you are a master chef or not; your kitchen is still one of the most important spaces in your home. In most cases, the kitchen functions as the hub of the house. It is where family members come together not just to feed their bellies but to nourish their souls as well. Irrespective of the physical size of the space available to you, your kitchen should be warm and inviting.

You may be getting the urge to skip this chapter altogether and get straight to the decluttering part but hold your horses! As Brian Tracy says, "Every minute you spend in planning saves 10 minutes in execution; this gives you a 1,000 percent Return on Energy!"

I am not the most patient person in the world, so, just like you, I often just want to get to the task instead of wasting any time on planning and strategizing. Over the years, I have learned that I end up exerting myself, but it's often not especially rewarding – I simply wasn't sufficiently organized. Without proper planning, your energies are not well directed and focused enough to achieve the goal. In fact, you may not even have enough clarity about the goal itself that you are trying to achieve.

I would highly recommend that you do all the exercises suggested in this chapter. Don't do them mentally but write them down on paper or digitally. I personally prefer to use a physical journal for these kinds of tasks as I find it easier to gain clarity on a subject when I am using an actual pen and paper. But even digitally is fine. You just need to put everything in writing, so you have a concrete plan to look at and follow. It will help you enormously as you go through the process of decluttering and reorganizing your kitchen.

Understand How Your Space is Used

In modern times, the kitchen is hardly ever used for just cooking. Think about it – your friend comes over to say hello. You offer to make her a steaming cup of hot chocolate. As you step inside the kitchen, she follows you to help you out but also because you are both wrapped in an interesting conversation. Before you know it, you've already spent several hours in the kitchen talking, discussing, and laughing together over a cup of hot chocolate.

There is a very special kind of drawing power that the kitchen has. It often compels families to huddle together thanks to the enveloping warmth and comfort it provides.

If you are a mother, perhaps you help your kids with their homework at the kitchen table while you are cooking. Maybe you live alone but the kitchen is where you find yourself working on your laptop or working through your finances. It's also possible that the kitchen is where you often sit down to make all your personal and professional phone calls.

While growing up, I often saw my father sitting at the kitchen table balancing checkbooks while talking to my mom. I remember bringing my broken toys to him and he would help me glue them together at the kitchen table.

The point I am trying to make here is that you must have a realistic understanding of how your kitchen is currently being used. Is it a space reserved exclusively for cooking occasional or regular meals (that's hardly ever the case), or does it function as the central hub of your dwelling?

How your kitchen is being used is going to be unique to you and your family. It is crucial that you develop a realistic understanding of it in order to plan this space well. Your kitchen should be aesthetically pleasing, functionally optimized, and efficient to run. Most importantly, it should serve you and your family's unique needs.

Exercise

Write down the answers to the following questions as honestly and realistically as possible. In other words, don't write what you wish were true for your kitchen but what is actually true for your kitchen at the moment. You can also ask these questions to your family members and ask for their input.

- How much time do you spend in your kitchen on an average day?

- How much time does the rest of your family spend in the kitchen on an average day?
- Is your kitchen used exclusively for cooking, or is it used for performing other activities as well? If it's a hub for other activities, then create a list of exactly what kind of things you and your family do in the kitchen.

Understanding the Space You Have Available to You

You can efficiently and aesthetically organize a space only when you understand it. Large and small are relative terms – what may be small for your large family could be a generously large kitchen space for a family of two. So I want you to assess the kind of space you have available to yourself. Is it big enough to meet all your needs, or does it feel too small and cluttered for everything you do there?

From my perspective, decluttering isn't something that is performed merely by eliminating unnecessary objects from a space. I feel it also involves eliminating things that are not relevant to that space. For instance, if you have too many books and notebooks lying on a kitchen table, it can make your space look cluttered. You can make your kitchen more organized instantly by removing those books and notebooks. You could easily shift them to another space that might be more suitable for studying. However, it depends on your situation. If you are a busy mother of two who wants to multitask to use her time most efficiently, then helping your kids with their homework while you're cooking is one of the best ways of doing it. If that's the case, you'll have to think about how you can utilize the kitchen space optimally.

Decluttering Your Kitchen in 5 Easy Steps

A space looks cluttered when it has objects unintentionally lying around that don't seem to be truly 'at home' there. For instance, a kitchen table used as a desktop is likely to make the kitchen look cluttered because the kitchen table is meant for a completely different activity. A lot of people who must do their desk work in the kitchen end up installing a proper desk and computer in one corner of the kitchen. You can consider this solution if it seems important to be able to perform such tasks in the kitchen.

Now, I want you to try something else out – try getting rid of everything that doesn't actually belong in the kitchen and look at how much space you have available. Does your kitchen feel large and spacious, or do you get the feeling that it is bursting at the seams?

I want you to have a good understanding of your starting point – this will help identify your problem areas. You'll understand better exactly which aspects of your kitchen are bothering you the most and that need to be addressed urgently.

Exercise

If you remove everything that doesn't actually belong in the kitchen and assess what you are left with, I would strongly recommend that you start by taking pictures of your kitchen. Do that before anything else. It will assist, not just as a reference for 'before' the makeover appearance, but also because photographing a space often helps us identify problem areas and issues that we otherwise miss.

Write down the answers to the following questions:

- What is the feeling that you get as soon as you enter your kitchen?
- Does your kitchen feel large and spacious or small and suffocating?
- Do you think you have too many visible things lying around? Are there too few? Or, perhaps, there are just enough?
- Which items are occupying the maximum amount of space in your kitchen? Do you and/or your family actually use these items? If yes, then how often are those items used?
- Does your kitchen require additional shelving units/drawers/organizers?
- What is bothering you most about your kitchen now?
- What do you think would be the best way of solving that problem, or what kind of solution would you most prefer for resolving that issue?

Visualize Your Space

Now is the time to start thinking about what you would like your kitchen to look and feel like. Remember, there is no right or wrong answer to this. If you want to work out of your kitchen table eight hours a day, that's totally fine. I am just suggesting that your kitchen space should be used intentionally and efficiently. So if you will be doing a lot of desk work, then as I suggested earlier, it would be best to get a compact but proper computer table installed in one corner.

Similarly, if your family spends a lot of time hanging out in the kitchen, then you can think of ways in which you can make it cozier, more relaxing and comfortable. Perhaps what you need more than anything are chairs that are truly comfortable?

You are the only person (and your family) who would know what works best for your kitchen.

Another important thing that you should do is measure each area before you begin working with it. This is a tip I learned from an interior designer many years ago. I had bought a couch that wouldn't go through the door of my apartment. My interior designer friend enlightened me about the importance of measuring your space before buying any new furniture or, for that matter, any item that will be occupying the space.

I would strongly recommend that you measure your kitchen to see how much actual space you have available to you. A self-retraction metal tape works best for getting accurate measurements. This exercise is going to come in handy in the organizing chapter when we will devise a plan for efficiently organizing your kitchen. For now, I just want you to get a general idea of how big or small your kitchen is by measuring the four sides of it.

Once you have developed a deeper understanding of the size of your kitchen, the next step is to create a vision for what you want it to look like. I advise you to follow the next exercise to assist you with this step.

Exercise

- Measure the four walls of the kitchen to get an idea of the overall space that is available to you.

- Look for images online of kitchens that are spatially similar to yours and observe how they have been organized.
- Collect images that inspire you – you can pin them to your Pinterest board or store them in an offline folder. You could also print them for inspiration.

Answer the following questions to develop greater clarity about what you would like your kitchen to look and feel like:

- What are the important tasks that I would continue to perform in my kitchen?
- What kind of feeling do I want my kitchen to evoke in me (and in my family members) every time I walk into it? (For instance, should it feel spacious, airy, or warm and cozy?)
- What kind of colors would I like to use in my kitchen?
- Which decor do I like best for my kitchen? (For instance, modern or vintage, classic or mid-century) If you aren't sure what this means, just look for images with the search term 'kitchen design style.'

Chapter 2
Decluttering the Kitchen

"The first step in crafting the life you want is to get rid of everything you don't."

— *Joshua Becker (Goodreads, n.d.)*

As I said in the previous chapter, the kitchen is often the hub of a home. It is where we spend a lot of time, whether cooking, conversing, or doing a host of other things. It's also one area of the house that is likely to become cluttered very quickly – thanks to the many cabinets and drawers most modern kitchens are equipped with.

The kitchen is also one place where we go a step further to justify hoarding different objects we don't really need. I mean, for instance, I counted a total of ten bottle openers when I was regularly reaching out for just one of the ten. Also, very often, our kitchen is designed and equipped with things we wish we were using but that aren't relevant to our current lifestyle. For example, I had a coffee maker occupying valuable real estate on my kitchen countertop when I hadn't had coffee in over a decade.

The process of decluttering isn't just a superficial attempt to rid our life of excesses – it is also a significant process of getting to know ourselves at a much deeper level. You can't declutter without understanding who you are and what your needs are. Of course, the same applies to understanding the needs and personalities of your family members if you are living with them.

When you are decluttering, you aren't just deciding what to keep and what to discard – you are also delving deeper into who you are and the life that you are leading. The better you understand yourself, the easier it is to declutter. According to a November 2020 Harvard study (Hicks, 2020), decluttering can contribute to feelings of well-being.

Four Boxes for the Decluttering Process

For the decluttering process, I strongly advise my clients to get four large cardboard boxes. Label each of them as:

Discard, Donate, Ponder, Fix

In the 'discard' box, you would place all the things that need to be discarded. Since there may be a lot of pantry items like expired food, you want to complete the discarding process as quickly as possible. Don't wait till the box is overflowing. The decluttering process may take you one day, or you could end up needing several days for it. There is nothing wrong with taking longer to complete the decluttering process. Just make sure that you empty the contents of this discard box every day, or at least that should be the ideal you aim for.

Decluttering Your Kitchen in 5 Easy Steps

The 'donate' box would contain items that aren't useful to you but which can be used by someone else. Again, as you are placing items in this box, you can decide mentally where and to whom you want to donate those items. If you want to donate the items to different people or at different locations, you can group the items together and place them in different plastic bags. Label them appropriately so you know which bag is meant for whom.

The third box, which I want you to label as 'ponder,' is part of what I like to call my Command-Z solution. If you have read my other books, then you must already be familiar with it. But for the uninitiated, here is a quick description of what goes in this box. This box would contain all those items that you are currently not using but you're also not ready to part with. It is like hitting command-z on your computer. If, at any point, you feel you are missing any of the items you have placed inside this box, you go back and rescue it. Hence, the discarding process can easily be undone if the need arises. Most of the time, I have found that I hardly remember the items I've placed in this box. Barring a few times, I've hardly ever rescued anything as part of the command-z solution.

I am quite sure you won't miss most of the items you place in this box. After a while, you can go through the items in there and discard and donate all the things that no longer serve you. If you really want to reacquire something back, then you can do so without guilt, as well. The only caveat is that you can do it only when you are truly missing the item. Don't rescue the items when you are going through everything and deciding whether they should be discarded, donated, or saved.

The fourth box would include all those items that you aren't ready to part with, but you also aren't able to use as they are not in a working condition. You are going to put only those items in this box that you intend to get fixed and then start using again. For every item you put into this box, I want you to also create a deadline for when you are going to get it fixed. Otherwise, you'll just be holding on to clutter.

Make note of each item you have put in there by writing the details in a diary (physical or digital), and then assign a deadline by which you must get it fixed. If you forget about the date or just don't end up getting it fixed for one reason or another (like if you realized it is actually beyond repair now), then you must discard that item immediately!

How to Decide What to Keep and What to Discard

Deciding what to keep and what to discard is quite simple – you keep what is useful to you and discard or donate what is not. Now, for kitchen items, this can be quite tricky. You can easily convince yourself that you may want to eat that breakfast granola that's been sitting on the shelf unopened for the last month. You have found another brand of granola that tastes a lot better, and now it seems hard to go back to the old one. But since you have spent money on it, you keep telling yourself that you'll eat it at some point, although there is no timeline for when that elusive 'some day' may arrive.

For most of the kitchen items, I have created a simple rule. I keep only those items that I am currently using or that I intend to use within three months. This rule works best for pantry items as food that is left unattended too often either develops worms or goes bad. In case of other kitchen items such as baking trays or other tools that end up being used once or twice a year, you can extend the timeline. I would still say that if you won't be using something within a year, you most likely don't need that thing. If you haven't used something in the last two years, then chances are you won't be using it any time soon.

Also, decluttering your kitchen can't be a one-off event. You have to regularly keep going through the items stocked up in your kitchen and decide whether they are serving a purpose or not. The kitchen is one of those areas of the house that is likely to become cluttered again right after you have decluttered it. That's why chapter one was so important. To prevent and tackle clutter on a regular basis, you need to have a good understanding of the vision you have for your kitchen and the lifestyle that you are currently leading.

Tackle One Area at a Time

You want to be able to maintain a relatively functional kitchen even while you are decluttering the space. Therefore, it is better to tackle one area at a time. Yes, you can go all in and declutter the entire kitchen in a day or two, but that's not realistic for a lot of people. You have to see what works best with your personal schedule and spend time decluttering accordingly.

For instance, on the first day, you can tackle one or two cabinets, the next day, you can do the cutlery drawers, and so on. There is no right or wrong way of doing this. Whatever fits in with your schedule is the best move for you.

I am often amazed by the things I find stored at the back of my cabinets – so many long-forgotten items that are already long past their shelf life! It is absolutely essential that you get every single item out of the space you are decluttering, clean the space properly (check out the next chapter for my cleaning tips and methods), and then put everything back.

I would recommend that you read the organizing chapter as well to make sure that you are placing everything back in an organized fashion. Alternatively, you can create a temporary storage solution (like placing everything that is supposed to belong in a specific area inside a cardboard box). In that case, you can wait for the next chapters and then follow the instructions for cleaning and organizing everything. This would work well for people who like to do only one thing at a time. So if you want to focus only on the decluttering for now, then place everything in some kind of a temporary storage.

Again, there is no right or wrong way of doing this. You have to take into account your lifestyle and the amount of time you have. If you must maintain a functional kitchen throughout the decluttering and organizing period, then it may be a better idea for you to read the other chapters also right away. For you, decluttering, cleaning, and organizing one area at a time will be a better strategy.

Things to Consider Getting Rid Of

To give you further clarity on which items you should definitely declutter from your kitchen, here are a few pointers.

Gadgets You Don't Use

I absolutely love kitchen gadgets. They make life easier by making cooking more efficient. However, a lot of times, we buy a gadget that is a pain to assemble. It is simply not worth taking it out and putting it together every time we need it for something. As a result, most of the time, the gadget just sits around occupying valuable real estate in the kitchen while a simple tool that can be easily pulled out ends up being frequently used.

I want to urge you to re-evaluate every single gadget you have in your kitchen. Which ones are you really using? How often are you using them? Is it a lot more time and energy efficient to grab a simple tool?

I am suggesting that you get rid of all the gadgets that aren't being used regularly. If you aren't ready to part with them right away, then at least shift them to the ponder box. In case you end up truly missing any of them, you can rescue the gadget and place it back in your kitchen. However, if the idea of rescuing it also feels like a lot of work and you'd much rather just use another tool because it is easier to reach and faster to use, then you definitely don't need that gadget!

Expired Food Items

I know this sounds like a no-brainer but it's amazing how many expired food items I see in people's homes. You want to go check the dates on all cans, spices, and packaged items to find anything that has passed the expiry date. Get rid of these items immediately.

When it comes to food items without an expiry date label, you can check online to get an idea of their shelf life. I would strongly recommend that, moving forward, you write down the date when an item has been added to a container. You can write the date in a subtle manner at the bottom of the container with a marker pen. Every time you refill the container, erase the previous date and write the new one.

Random Lids and Jars

While jars with missing lids can be put to different uses, random lids hardly serve any purpose. I would suggest that you get rid of all the lids that don't match with a container. As for jars and other containers without a lid, see if you can actually put them to good use (like using them as a vase, a pencil holder, a spatula holder, etc.). If not, then get rid of them right away.

Damaged Dishes

Get rid of all chipped china, broken/cracked plates, and damaged glassware. Don't try to think of innovative ways to use them. It is best to purge them right away!

Extra Tools

More often than not, we own far too many kitchen tools. Honestly assess which tools you are actually using and purge the ones that don't get utilized. I know it can be hard to get rid of them as you think you may just need them at some point. Trust me, too many tools only prevent you from accessing the items that you genuinely need.

How many spatulas do you really need and which ones are you actually using? How many egg whisks do you need? Ask yourself this question for every single kitchen tool. Purge or ponder over all the tools that are under-utilized or simply never used.

Too Many Cleaning Supplies

Most of the time, the under-sink area is often a chaotic disaster. Take a look at your cleaning supplies and assess which ones you are really using. Get rid of any expired cleaning products and empty bottles/containers that are still sitting around. Try to pare down your cleaning supplies to the essentials that you are using most of the time.

The Chest Freezer

If you are anything like me, you also probably have a chest freezer where you store frozen food items. I use mine to store food items that I buy in bulk. I keep transferring them to the regular refrigerator freezer once I open them. The chest freezer is where I store my backup food or anything I don't use very frequently, such as ice cream jugs.

Honestly, the chest freezer is often a clutter magnet. It is very easy to overfill it with food that won't ever be used or items that we end up buying too many of simply because they were on sale.

To kickstart the decluttering process, I want you to go through each item that is currently there. Throw away any food item that has gone bad. I know a lot of items in the freezer can be consumed beyond the expiry date, but many times the food just doesn't taste good anymore as it loses flavor and texture. You have to use your discretion to decide if something is still good to be used or not. For example, there have been times when I left frozen pizza in there for too long – alright, I'll admit it, I put it in the freezer and totally forgot it was there. When I tried eating it after a very long time, the crust had become very hard and dry – it tasted like I was eating a styrofoam board.

If you want to be extra safe, then stick with the expiry date on the packet. After all, better safe than sorry! Also, when it comes to ice cream, you should definitely stick to the expiry date on the pack.

In case you have a lot of items that you bought on sale, you may have bought things that you and your family seldom eat. If you find any food item that you never actually consume and you're saving it for a day when you might want to eat such a food item, but you know that's never going to happen, just donate it.

Of course, there is a storage issue here; you can't risk keeping the donation pile sitting around for too long. Ask your neighbor if they have any need for it or immediately drive to the nearest food bank and drop it off there. Resist the temptation of putting it back into the freezer, thinking you'll do this another day. You'll likely end up never doing it. Also, be careful when donating frozen food that is way past the expiry date – others may not be open to receiving it.

You may discover some items that should be in your refrigerator's freezer right now – I know I often forget what I have lying around in the chest freezer. Moving forward, you really need to practice enough self-discipline to cut out the excess that you don't truly need. Discounts are great, but they end up being a waste of money if you are buying too many things you don't need or are never going to use!

Chapter 3

Cleaning the Kitchen

"When your environment is clean you feel happy motivated and healthy."

— *Lailah Gifty Akita (Think Great, Be Great!, 2014)*

Once you have finished decluttering the entire kitchen or a small section of it, it is time to deep clean that space. In this chapter, I am going to give you all the knowledge and instructions you need to clean your kitchen thoroughly. You can start incorporating these cleaning techniques, ideas, and methods into your day-to-day life. The whole point of cleaning regularly is so that you never reach a point when you have so much cleaning to do that it begins to feel like an overwhelming task.

At the end of the chapter, I will share with you good kitchen hygiene habits that you should definitely incorporate into your life. Your kitchen isn't just a space for preparing food; it is the hub of your home – the center from where you and all your family members derive their nourishment. This space should be treated with utmost respect and should be as efficiently functional as possible.

Prepare a Cleaning Caddy

You don't want to have to search all over the place to gather all your cleaning supplies every time you need them. Having all your cleaning supplies neatly stored in a caddy can cut down cleaning time further. You can easily gather all your supplies and get down to business whenever need be.

Also, I strongly believe in aesthetics combined with functionality. Who wants to reach for that ugly blue bucket and rotting sponge – that kind of thing makes your heart sink! You start thinking of cleaning as some kind of punishment. Make your cleaning caddy look as pretty as possible. I would suggest decanting the cleaning supplies into clear bottles. You can label them with chalkboard marker stickers that can be easily bought at any crafts store or online. Try to make your cleaning rags and gloves color coordinated.

I have managed to create a cleaning caddy that is a delight to look at. I would strongly advise that you keep your cleaning tools and supplies stored together in a caddy that can easily be carried around. You can easily buy a caddy with handles online or at your local home goods store. Now, let us discuss in detail the essentials that should be there in your cleaning caddy.

Microfiber Cloths

If you haven't yet gotten your hands on microfiber cloths, then you must acquire them right away! These soft rags act like mini-vacuum cleaners. They are extremely efficient at picking up dust from the surfaces they come in contact with. They work efficiently whether they are used wet or dry.

Cleaning Gloves

That's a no-brainer! We all know that cleaning can take a heavy toll on your hands. Use gloves for all cleaning tasks. You can also apply some heavy hand cream before placing your hands in the gloves. This will allow the moisture to seep much deeper into your skin while you are busy scrubbing the place.

Toothbrushes

Toothbrushes are an indispensable tool in any cleaning kit. You can buy them inexpensively at the local discount store. Just make sure that you are buying the soft-bristled ones. Keep separate toothbrushes for different cleaning jobs. You can label each one with a permanent marker. In my case, I have a dedicated brush for polishing silver, another one for cleaning around bathroom faucets, a separate toothbrush for scrubbing the kitchen faucet, and so on.

Cleaning Products

You don't need too many different types of cleansers. All you need is one glass cleaner and one multi-purpose cleaner. You can make your own DIY glass cleaner by mixing one cup of white vinegar with one cup of water and one cup of rubbing alcohol. For the all-purpose cleaner, skip the alcohol and mix one cup of white vinegar with one cup of water. You can also add a few drops of your favorite essential oil to the mix.

Cloths and Rags

Separate cloths and rags should be used for different kitchen cleaning purposes. A few rags should be set aside for cleaning up spills and washing the floors.

You should also have a few cloths and rags set aside for extremely dirty jobs. For instance, you can have a few for cleaning up nasty spills. Don't worry about keeping these rags and cloths stain-free.

Other Essential Kitchen Supplies

Apart from the cleaning caddy, you also need dishcloths in the kitchen for drying dishes and for wiping sinks, countertops, and tabletops. Make sure that you keep a separate dishcloth for each job. Hand towels should also be kept around to wipe hands while performing tasks.

Fine linen can be used for drying and polishing glassware, china, crystal, and silver. Make sure you have plenty of towels, cloths, and rags in your kitchen for all these different purposes. They should not be thrown in with the regular laundry. You can run your cleaning supplies in a separate load. If possible, don't wash the cloths, rags, and towels you have set aside for heavy-duty tasks with the ones that are meant for light cleaning purposes.

Start Cleaning

After completely decluttering a space, you must take the time to clean it thoroughly. Wipe all shelves, baseboard, cupboard doors, and other surfaces with the all-purpose cleaner using a microfiber cloth. Once the surfaces are dry, wipe them again with a dry cloth to ensure no dirt or debris remains.

Clean the kitchen windows and doors. Don't forget to wipe doorknobs and door handles, as well. Again, wipe first with a wet cloth and then, later on, with a dry cloth. Vacuum the floors and then use a wet mop to remove any dirt that may remain behind. Microfiber mops are much more efficient at cleaning than regular mops.

Cleaning the Dishes

Before you get to organizing your dishes, you must clean them thoroughly (especially the ones that haven't been used in a while). If you are washing the dishes by hand, then start with those dishes that are least soiled, and then progress on to the most heavily soiled ones. This means you would likely begin with glass, silver, and flatware. Be sure to use hot, sudsy water to clean the dishes.

To prevent breakage, wash similar items together. Glasses and plates, for example, should be washed separately from heavy pots and pans. For delicate or valuable items, wash only one item at a time.

If you want to wash the dishes in the dishwasher, then be sure to scrape off any hardened food debris that may be stuck on them. I would strongly recommend that you rinse all dishes before placing them in the dishwasher. This prevents utensils from aging prematurely; they won't get damaged by the excess friction caused by food particles flying around in the dishwasher.

You also want to place delicate and heat-vulnerable items on the top rack of the dishwasher and never on the lower rack. Follow the instructions on the dishwasher's user manual to prevent damaging your dishes and dishwasher.

Cleaning the Refrigerator

This is one area of the kitchen that often doesn't receive as much attention as it deserves. Since fresh food is stored in the refrigerator, there's always a chance of germs accumulating due to accidental spills, spoiled food, developing mold, etc.

Go through all the contents of your refrigerator (including the freezer and the vegetable drawer) and throw away anything that has gone bad. Get rid of any rotting piece of fruit or vegetable. One rotten piece can ruin the entire bunch.

Remove the shelves and drawers of the refrigerator. Club highly perishable items together and place them on one or two shelves that you leave inside the refrigerator. Place the remaining (not highly perishable) food items on the kitchen countertop.

Wash the shelves and drawers thoroughly with hot soapy water. Rinse and dry them. Wipe the surface of the refrigerator where they will be placed and then place them back. Shift the highly perishable items to the clean shelves and wash the shelf they had been standing on.

Don't use hot water on cold glass shelves – they may crack. Use any all-purpose cleaner to wipe the surfaces clean. For deodorizing the refrigerator, you can use baking soda. Add two tablespoons of baking soda to 500ml water and use the mixture to wipe the refrigerator surfaces.

Use these same suggestions to clean the freezer and chest freezer if you own one. Just make sure that you defrost the freezer, following the manufacturer's instructions, prior to the deep cleaning. If you have two freezers, then you can transfer as many food items to the other freezer as possible while doing the cleaning. Alternatively, you can preserve the food in an ice chest while cleaning the freezer.

Cleaning Stoves and Ovens

If you have a gas stove, remove the burner pans and burner grates. In the case of an electric stove, remove the heating elements and the reflector bowls underneath them. Soak the burner pans/grates/reflector bowls (except the heating elements of an electric stove) in a mixture of hot water and dishwashing liquid. After 15-20 minutes, wash them thoroughly and set them aside to dry. The heating elements need only be wiped with a well-wrung damp cloth (make sure that you are wiping them only when they are completely cool).

Wipe the stovetop with a solution of hot water and liquid detergent. If there are any stubborn food particles stuck on the stove surface, you can dampen them and allow them to stand until they soften. Once the stove is completely clean, replace the burner pans, grates, and reflector bowls. Wipe the exterior of the oven door and other accessible parts of the stovetop with the same mixture.

Most ovens these days have a self-cleaning mechanism. Don't use detergent inside the oven or you could end up destroying the self-cleaning mechanism of the oven surfaces. For cleaning the oven properly, it's best to follow the instruction manual that came with it. In case you have a non-self-cleaning oven, it would be best to buy a commercial oven cleaner and use it as advised by the manufacturer.

The broiling pan used in the oven is often safe for dishwashers and can be cleaned in the same way you would clean a soiled pan.

Cleaning the Microwave

Commercial oven cleaners should never be used inside a microwave. Use a cloth dipped in warm, sudsy water (any mild liquid detergent will work) to wipe off all surfaces. Be sure to wipe all surfaces, including the top, bottom, sides, and both sides of the door. Clean the door seals and seams as well.

Daily Kitchen Cleaning Routine and Habits to Incorporate

- Clean and tidy the kitchen as you are cooking. Don't leave it for when you finish cooking.
- Wash ALL the dishes – load the dishes in the dishwasher and/or hand wash them before going to bed.
- Clean the sink after each use (using warm water and dishwashing liquid). Wipe the sink with a cloth dedicated for that purpose – your goal should be a fresh, sparkling, dry sink at all times.
- Every morning, or as soon as the dishes have dried, place them back in their spot.
- Wipe kitchen countertops and stovetops (wipe the burners and baskets without removing them).
- Sweep kitchen floor.
- Wipe the kitchen table.
- Change kitchen towels daily.
- Clean all spills immediately – don't allow them to dry up.
- Throw away anything in the refrigerator that has turned moldy, smelly, spotty, or slimy.
- Take the trash out.

Weekly Kitchen Cleaning Routine

- Go through all the contents of the refrigerator (best done immediately or a day before the weekly grocery shopping).
- Wash the refrigerator.
- Take burner pans and burner grates off gas stoves to clean them thoroughly.
- Launder all kitchen cloths, towels, and rags.
- Clean all other kitchen appliances.
- Sanitize your sponges – microwave them on high heat for one minute.
- Mop the kitchen floor.
- Wipe all cabinet doors and handles.
- Wipe kitchen door, windows, and handles.
- Clean the garbage disposal unit (follow manufacturer's instructions).

Monthly Kitchen Cleaning Routine

- Deep clean all cabinets, cupboards, and drawers.
- Go through all pantry items – discard all expired food.
- Clean and sanitize trash/recycling bins.
- Deep clean the dishwasher (follow manufacturer's instructions).
- Wash kitchen rugs (if you have any).
- Dust and wipe all light fixtures.

To Be Done When Needed Kitchen Cleaning Routine

- Deep clean the oven.
- Clean under the refrigerator.
- Declutter, clean, and organize all kitchen tools.
- Repair or replace damaged tools as needed.
- Defrost and deep clean the freezer.

Chapter 4
Organizing the Kitchen

"Being organized isn't about getting rid of everything you own or trying to become a different person: it's about living the way you want to live, but better."

— *Andrew Mellen (Thought for Today - Organization, n.d.)*

Now that you have finished decluttering and cleaning, it's time to start organizing the kitchen! Again, if you have a large kitchen or you're simply short on time, then you want to complete this task bit-by-bit, tackling one small area at a time.

If you are doing the entire kitchen in one go, then it's best, I would say, that you begin the organization project with your refrigerator. This is so that you can put back all perishable items immediately.

Refrigerator

The open shelving space inside the refrigerator can quickly turn into a total disaster zone if you aren't intentional with your organizing. Moving forward, don't store anything randomly. Every item should belong to a category, and there should be a container for storing items belonging to that category.

You want to invest in good-quality clear plastic bins designed specifically for the refrigerator. An ordinary organizer won't do the job; you want to make sure that the material can withstand constant cold temperatures inside the refrigerator.

These organizer bins come in a host of different shapes and sizes. You can buy several different shapes and sizes for variety. To maximize the vertical space inside the refrigerator, you can also buy sliding drawers that can easily be attached to the shelf. You might also get a drawer that is designed specifically for eggs in case you have a lot of eggs to store.

These clear containers can be used for versatile purposes. For instance, one week, you may use a bin to store fresh fruits and another week for keeping your leftover turkey sandwich safe. You also want to store together items that you would use at the same time. For example, store sandwich ingredients together (in other words, club together the meat, sauces/spreads, and cheese) so that you can easily assemble a sandwich without having to rummage through the entire refrigerator for 10-15 minutes.

The key to an organized refrigerator lies in limiting the open shelf space. Only those items that are too large and bulky to be stored in any of the bins should be stored in the open shelf space. A large milk or juice jug may not fit anywhere else.

Similarly, if you are storing pre-cut vegetables in large jars, they might fit better in the open shelf space.

To make your refrigerator more aesthetically pleasing, I would suggest getting rid of food packaging. Store everything in clear glass or plastic containers. You can use dishwasher-safe chalkboard labels (easily available online or at any local crafts store) to note down the item name and the expiry date.

Here are some more tips for making your refrigerator more organized and aesthetically pleasing:

- Use stackable wine racks for storing wine bottles.
- Use waterproof refrigerator mats to line the shelves and drawers of your refrigerator (this will make cleaning a lot easier as you can remove the mats and wash them separately – no need to remove the shelves and drawers every week. You can clean them once every couple of months by taking everything out).
- Store leftovers in glass storage boxes.

Again, minimizing the packaging material is the best way to make your refrigerator look neat and attractive. Your refrigerator should be a delightful sight to behold every time you open the door.

How to Utilize the Shelves and Drawers in Your Refrigerator

The top shelf is the warmest shelf in your refrigerator. Use it for storing leftovers, snacks, and other items that you intend to eat soon. Don't use it for storing fresh meat.

The middle shelf enjoys consistently cooler temperatures. Use it for storing items that are likely to spoil easily. For instance, milk and eggs. Since this shelf usually has the maximum amount of vertical shelving space, it can be used for storing taller containers.

The bottom shelf is the coolest spot in your refrigerator. Use it for storing meat and other items that must be kept at consistently low temperatures.

The bottom drawers are usually dedicated to storing fruits and vegetables. Just make sure you are storing fruits and vegetables separately because the ethylene emitted by fruits can cause vegetables to spoil prematurely.

The door is the warmest part of your refrigerator. You should definitely not store eggs here. It is ideal for storing condiments that are high in salt and/or vinegar. You can also store jams and jellies here.

Freezer and Chest Freezer

If you aren't using some kind of an organizer in the freezer, then you are guaranteed to end up with a jumbled mess. I personally love using freezer-safe clear boxes to keep similar items together. I would strongly recommend that you label each box. You can stack them on top of one another.

In the case of the chest freezer, you can also use crates, baskets, or maybe even cardboard boxes (if you are on a budget). The point is to create a clear demarcation of space and keep similar things grouped with items in the same category.

Another very important thing for keeping the freezer organized is to maintain an inventory. Keep stock of exactly what items are stored in the freezer and the chest freezer. Every time you pull something out of either of the two, update the inventory. If you are moving something from the chest freezer to the refrigerator's freezer, then that needs to be updated accordingly as well. This will help you keep track of the items you currently have and what you are running low on. That way, you'll be able to restock it in a timely manner.

Each of your freezers should have a separate inventory. Train your family to update the inventory every time they pull something out of the freezer, as well.

Pantry

Your pantry should be organized in such a way that you can quickly put away groceries after returning from the store. Everything should be clearly visible and easily accessible; that way, you don't have to figure out what's inside which container.

I would advise you to measure your pantry space (both the length and the width) to know the exact dimensions you're working with. Don't skip this step – it will really help out with planning your pantry layout. Knowing the exact dimensions of your space will help you determine the size and number of organizers you need in it.

Write down the different sections you need to create for separate categories of food. For instance, you can have sections like ready-to-eat snacks, breakfast cereals, baking goods, etc. How many sections you need to create in your pantry will depend entirely upon your unique needs. To decide which sections you need, you can also run through an entire day in your head – see what you and your family are eating throughout the course of the day.

Once you have decided the number of sections you need and you're familiar with the total pantry area available to you, it's time to select your storage containers. Take into consideration the total number of items you generally have for each category of food, and then create an estimate for the number of jars, bins, and baskets you are going to need.

I am a strong proponent of using clear containers in the pantry. Getting rid of the original packaging in which the food comes is essential for making your pantry look aesthetically pleasing. Besides, when everything is placed inside clear containers, you can easily see exactly what items you have available. I recommend writing the expiry date for each item at the bottom of the clear container. You can use a marker pen that can easily be erased using a glass cleaner.

If you want to make your pantry look like the ones from home decor magazines, it's best that you store only one size and style of storage containers in each area. For example, you can store all your rice and beans in one section using glass jars that are the same size and height. This makes everything look very uniform and neat.

To keep all the containers visible, you can place the ones at the back of the shelf on a wooden block. Use wooden blocks to create separate rows of containers so they can be visible according to their cascading height – the tallest ones at the back should be raised the highest. The ones in front of them should be slightly lower, and the height of the blocks should descend consistently. The front row containers should be placed directly on the shelf and should be the lowest ones in the order of height.

To make the food items even easier to access, you can label the containers. Use a label maker to create professional-looking labels. Alternatively, you can buy chalkboard stickers and manually label each container.

Spices

I personally like to use a drawer organizer for storing all my spices in alphabetical order. I write the expiry date at the bottom of each jar. If you have a drawer that you can dedicate to spices, then you can buy a tiered rack that would fit into the drawer.

You can also install a wall-mounted rack or a sliding spice rack inside your cabinet. Some people also like to store their spices on a lazy Susan style of organizer. There are indeed many options available in the market. You can get one that suits your space and your style the best.

Again, storing the spices and herbs in the same size/type of containers helps keep everything looking neat. The labeling should also be consistent – use the same type and style of labeling to make sure everything looks uniform.

Cooking Tools and Serving Utensils

It can be hard to find the right cooking tool when you have an overabundance of utensils. I hope you took the decluttering aspect very seriously and have now pared down to the tools you actually use. I like to store my cooking tools close to the stove so that I can grab what I need easily while preparing food. The tools I don't use that often (like baking tools) are stored in another drawer that is less easily accessible. Serving utensils are stored in another drawer that is also close to the stove so I can quickly grab the right tools when I am getting ready to serve the food.

I like using expandable drawer organizers for storing cooking tools, serving utensils, and cutlery. You can get them in plastic or bamboo material. I personally prefer the bamboo organizer. You can also get a utensil holder for storing your kitchen tools near the stovetop. I like to keep my countertop as clean and uncluttered as possible. Hence, I prefer storing everything in closed drawers, cabinets, and cupboards.

Pots and Pans

I know that most people just stack pots and pans on top of one another. I personally detest this as I have to dig out the one I need every time I'm cooking. Also, this method causes a lot of wear and tear to your utensils. I would recommend investing in pots and pans organizer racks that can easily be stored inside cabinets. It's not a huge space saver, but it does help elongate the life of your utensils. It also makes pulling out the right pot or pan very easy and convenient.

I like to keep the lid and pot or pan together. This way, I can pull both of them out in one go. May not seem like much, but as a busy mother and wife, I'm grateful for even the smallest amount of time I manage to save throughout the day!

Dishes

I like to store my plates in vertical plate holders. I stack smaller plates together and larger plates as a separate section of their own. I place bowls of the same size one on top of the other. To maximize the shelf space in cabinets, I use shelf racks. This way, I can organize mugs, bowls, and other dishes in a tiered fashion.

Depending upon the type of space available to you, you can go two ways. Get a shelf rack that can be placed anywhere in the cabinet or even on the countertop if you wish. Or you can get a two-tiered corner shelf rack that will help maximize the corner space you have available.

For wine glasses, you can buy an under-cabinet wine glass holder shelf. This way, all the glasses are easily accessible while occupying limited space in your kitchen cabinets. When it comes to storing glasses without a stem, you can place them on the shelf, or you can store them on a glass drying rack.

Kitchen Gadgets

I know how tempting it is to buy lots of different gadgets. But, to be honest, the idea that they make life easier for you is something of an illusion. Most people have too many gadgets that they never use. I would suggest that you pare down to the bare essentials – keep only those gadgets around that you use regularly.

Again, I am not a fan of storing things on the kitchen countertop. I like to store my gadgets in organizer bins inside closed cabinets. The gadgets that you rarely use but are not ready to part with can be stored away from the cooking area on the top shelf of a cabinet at the back.

I hope you enjoyed all the kitchen organization hacks I shared with you in this chapter. Organization shouldn't be something that you do only once and then forget about. You have to regularly keep repeating the process of decluttering, cleaning, and organizing. That's especially true when we are talking about a space that is as dynamic as the kitchen. You also don't have to get everything on point right away. Over time, you can further refine your system and become more organized – just do what you are able to do right now because that is good enough!

Chapter 5
Meal Planning

"View health as an investment, not an expense."

— *John Quelch (BrainyQuote, n.d.)*

If you want to do anything well in life, you need a plan for exactly how you'll go about it. Hence, if you want to feed wholesome, nourishing food to yourself and your family, then you need to plan all your meals ahead of time. After all, standing in front of the refrigerator wondering what you can cook this evening isn't the most productive use of time. Worse still, you may start preparing a meal and then realize you are short on several ingredients. We have all been through that nightmare when we drove to the grocery store just to get one key ingredient that was missing from our repertoire, only to come back home and realize that we need to run back to the store to get another ingredient we don't have at hand!

Creating a Meal Plan

I generally go through all my refrigerator items once a week. I also try to wash and wipe all the shelf liners and organizer baskets after removing any food item that's gone bad. While I am doing the culling, I am also noting down the items I need to restock. By the end of the refrigerator purge, I have a list of items that need to be bought for the week.

Once I am done with the refrigerator, I sit down to create a menu plan for the week. I know there are many kinds of fancy planners available for it these days, but I use a regular notebook to write down what I am planning to prepare for breakfast, lunch, and dinner each day of the week. You can also do this digitally if you prefer, but I prefer to write things on paper the old-fashioned way. It helps me to think more clearly, and I simply tend to plan better on paper.

After preparing the menu for the week, I write down the ingredients that would be needed for each meal, marking anything that is currently not available in my kitchen. You don't have to write the ingredient list every single time. What I realized is that I prepare the same kind of dishes in rotation. I have prepared a separate recipe card for each dish. I refer to this card and make note of any ingredient that is currently not available in my kitchen. All such items get added to my grocery shopping list for the week.

If you don't want to prepare a meal plan for the entire week, then you can also do it for the next 2-3 days or whatever works best for you. For me and for most people, planning everything in one go for the entire week works better. I am able to do my grocery shopping once a week, and one trip to the market proves sufficient to supply me with all the essentials for that week. If you're going to do the meal planning every couple of days, then you'll also have to factor in more visits to the grocery store since you're likely going to be short on at least some of the ingredients required for the meals.

Shopping for Food

I like to patronize the same shops in my locality frequently. Over time, I have managed to develop a rapport with the staff there, so they're better able to assist me with my needs. I am also well familiar with all the shelves and sections in those shops, so I don't waste much time when I go there.

While shopping, it is best to start with non-perishable items like canned, bottled, and any other packaged item that doesn't need to be stored in the refrigerator or freezer. That would include items like breakfast cereals, rice, beans, pasta, etc. Next up, I like to stock up on refrigerated items like cheese, meat, poultry, milk, fruits, vegetables, etc.

At the very end, I load up my cart with any frozen food or hot cooked item that I may be buying. Make sure that you aren't picking any frozen food that has been left lying above the freezer line where there's a chance of it going bad. It also goes without saying (but I'll say it anyway!) that you want to carefully check the packaging and expiry date of each item before placing it in your cart.

You should also ensure that you are placing all the items in your cart according to their temperature. So, for instance, items at room temperature should be grouped together, cold/frozen items should be placed near each other, and any hot food should be kept with other hot items only.

During the bagging process, make sure that the hot and cold items are bagged separately. Meats, poultry, and any other food item that may drip raw juices or liquids should be placed inside an extra layer of plastic bag. This way, the drips won't fall on other food items. Avoid buying packets that are dripping in the first place, but if it starts happening after you have made the purchase, placing them inside an additional plastic bag is your best bet.

If you are planning to run other errands on the same day that you go grocery shopping, try to shop for food at the end of your trip. Post-grocery shopping, try to get back home as fast as possible. When the weather is hot, place the groceries in the passenger area of your car and keep the air conditioner switched on. If you must take a detour before coming back home, then you can take a portable ice chest with you before heading out to the grocery store.

Put food away right after you return from the store. Be sure to tackle hot, frozen, or cold food items first. Store them at the appropriate temperature.

Note: I want to include a word of caution here. Thanks to the overabundance of food in our 'modern' lives, it can be tempting to buy more food than we need, especially if we find something on sale. Don't get me wrong – I am myself obsessed with finding great bargains and discounts, but I have had to learn to draw the line. It is tempting to buy ten boxes of strawberries because they are for sale at $1 each, but what's the point if I can't finish them and they start going bad by the following day? If you think about it, instead of being a money saver, such a fear actually ends up as a significant waste.

Besides, when you buy things like microwaveable pizza on sale, you feel obliged to finish all of it even though you already started feeling full after two slices. You can end up overeating by consuming excess calories simply because you didn't want to waste the pizza and you think you should get your money's worth.

I want you to start being more disciplined with your purchases. Don't buy things you or your family are unlikely to eat within their expiry period just because they're on sale. Stick to your original grocery list that you prepared after creating your weekly meal plan. It will help you remain focused. In the long run, you'll eat healthier and save more money. A lot of bargains are not really bargains when you factor in their long-term impact on your health and wallet. But if you find something at a bargain price that you will definitely be eating (and you are sure it will be consumed within its expiration period), then by all means go for it!

Meal Prep in Advance

You can save time by prepping for the next day's meal while cooking dinner the night before. This could mean chopping the onions, peeling the cucumbers or carrots, and mixing the marinade for the chicken. Whatever kind of meal it will be, start preparing for it as much in advance as possible.

You can classify one area of your refrigerator as the meal prep section. You can use a refrigerator-safe tray for separating this section. This is where you'll store all the prepped items. I like to use clear click-and-lock style food containers for all the chopped vegetables and fruits. For liquids, I like to use mason jars. I would advise you to get containers in different sizes to accommodate the various quantities of prepped items your recipes may require.

When you have prepped in advance, it is a lot easier to do the cooking when mealtime approaches. No matter how tired you are, you can find some energy to cook when all the toughest jobs have already been dealt with.

Conclusion

I hope you have enjoyed reading this book as much as I have loved writing it. I hope you have taken all the action steps I have highlighted throughout this book and now you are able to enjoy a kitchen that is functional while also being aesthetically pleasing.

If you haven't done everything, then go back to chapter 1 and start the process all over again. You can do it! I believe in you – you must also believe in yourself. Slowly, one step at a time, you'll get to the final destination.

Lastly, I want to remind you that decluttering, cleaning, and organizing are not things we do once in a while. To live a beautiful life, we must incorporate these three into our daily routines. They should feel more like a natural way of life than tasks to be accomplished within a certain time frame.

It you want to learn more about decluttering, check out my my book, *Decluttering Workbook: The Essential Guide to Organize and Declutter Your Home and Life With Exercises and Checklists.*

Conclusion

Once again, thank you for placing your trust in me. Wishing you a beautiful kitchen, a lovely home, and great health for the rest of your life!

Lisa

Thank You

Thank you for purchasing my book.

You chose this book. Thank you for picking it! And thanks for reading it all the way through. I hope you received value from the book and found the decluttering advice to be helpful.

Could you please consider writing a review of my book on the platform?

Writing a review is the best and easiest way to support people like me who self-publish books. Your review helps other people find my work and enjoy it, too!

It will help me write the kind of books that will help you get the results you want. It would mean a lot to me to hear from you.

>> **Leave a review on Amazon US** <<
>> **Leave a review on Amazon UK** <<

References

110 Bob Proctor quotes from the inspirational self-help author. Free Ideas For Family Fun & Learning. (n.d.). Retrieved March 30, 2022, from https://kidadl.com/articles/bob-proctor-quotes-from-the-inspirational-self-help-author

28 amazing quotes that will inspire you to get organized. Order Your Life. (2018, February 1). Retrieved March 31, 2022, from https://orderyourlife.com/blogs/blog/28-amazing-quotes-that-will-inspire-you-to-get-organized

Aarssen, C. (2020). *The Declutter Challenge.* Mango Publishing Group. p. 1.

Abramson, A. (2019, September 3). *10 quotes that will empower you to declutter anything.* Apartment Therapy. Retrieved March 30, 2022, from https://www.apartmenttherapy.com/inspirational-quotes-decluttering-36638725

Akita, L. G. (2014). *Think Great, Be Great!* (Vol. 1). CreateSpace Independent Publishing Platform; Edition 1.

References

A thing worth doing. Society of Gilbert Keith Chesterton. (2012, April 29). Retrieved March 30, 2022, from https://www.chesterton.org/a-thing-worth-doing/

Becker, J. (2019). *The Minimalist Home*. Waterbook. p. 22.

Becker, J. (n.d.). *Joshua Becker*. Goodreads. Retrieved May 10, 2022, from https://www.goodreads.com/quotes/7048262-the-first-step-in-crafting-the-life-you-want-is

Benjamin Franklin. BrainyQuote. (n.d.). Retrieved May 10, 2022, from https://www.brainyquote.com/quotes/benjamin_franklin_138217

Bray, G. (2019). *The Organized Mum Method*. Piatkus. p. 8.

Cirillo, F. (2018). *The pomodoro technique.* Random House UK.

Cleaning. Wikipedia. (2022, February 28). Retrieved March 31, 2022, from https://en.wikipedia.org/wiki/Cleaning

Clear, J. (2020, February 4). *How long does it actually take to form a new habit?* JamesClear.com. Retrieved March 31, 2022, from https://jamesclear.com/new-habit

Crombie, L. (2021). *The 15-minute Clean*. Welbeck.

Dunham, D. (2016). *The Silent Land*. Matador.

Fields Millburn, J., & Nicodemus, R. (2019, August 7). *Getting rid of just-in-case items: 20 dollars, 20 minutes.* The Minimalists. Retrieved March 31, 2022, from https://www.theminimalists.com/jic/

References

Filippelli, G. (2019, July 20). Perspective | how the dust in your home may affect your health. *The Washington Post*. Retrieved December 23, 2021, from https://www.washingtonpost.com/health/how-the-dust-in-your-home-may-affect-your-health/2019/07/19/9f716068-a351-11e9-bd56-eac6bb02d01d_story.html

Habit quotes. Brainy Quote. (n.d.). Retrieved March 31, 2022 from https://www.brainyquote.com/topics/habit-quotes

Hage, J. (2021, November 24). *Motivational quotes for cleaning: 20 positive clean home sayings.* Filling the Jars. Retrieved March 31, 2022, from https://www.fillingthejars.com/motivational-quotes-for-cleaning

Hallowell, E. (2006). *Crazy Busy*. Ballantine Books.

Hicks, D. C. (2020, November). *Understanding well-being: Clearing Personal Space For Wellness*. Harvard Library Office for Scholarly Communication. Retrieved May 10, 2022, from https://dash.harvard.edu/handle/1/37365612

Kondo, M. (2020). *Tidying up with Marie Kondo*. Ten Speed Press. p. 21.

Lao Tzu quote. Brainy Quote. (n.d.). Retrieved March 30, 2022 from https://www.brainyquote.com/quotes/lao_tzu_137141

Mackey, M. (2022, January 13). *100 quotes about self-care, because being good to yourself has never been more important.* Parade. Retrieved March 31, 2022, from https://parade.com/1070248/maureenmackey/self-care-quotes/

References

Mellen, A. (n.d.). *Thought for Today - Organization*. Oprah.com. Retrieved May 10, 2022, from https://www.oprah.com/spirit/thought-for-today-quotes-on-organization/all

Nelson, M. (2004). *Stop Clutter From Stealing Your Life*. New Page Books.

Night, B. (2013). *The Art of Minimalist Organization*. Self published.

Our favorite clutter quotes: Unmade decisions and procrastination. Postconsumers. (2020, August 24). Retrieved March 30, 2022, from https://www.postconsumers.com/2015/01/09/clutter-quotes-6/

Pathak, A. (2021, August 27). *150 epic goal setting quotes that will change your life.* Vantage Circle HR Blog. Retrieved March 30, 2022, from https://blog.vantagecircle.com/goal-setting-quotes/

Quelch, J. (n.d.). *John Quelch quotes*. BrainyQuote. Retrieved May 10, 2022, from https://www.brainyquote.com/quotes/john_quelch_757984

Routine quotes. BrainyQuote. (n.d.). Retrieved March 31, 2022, from https://www.brainyquote.com/topics/routine-quotes

Smart criteria. Wikipedia. (2022, February 24). Retrieved March 30, 2022, from https://en.wikipedia.org/wiki/SMART_criteria

Smith, M. (2018). *Cozy Minimalist Home*. Zondervan.

Tidy. Cambridge English Dictionary. (n.d.). Retrieved March

References

31, 2022, from https://dictionary.cambridge.org/dictionary/english/tidy

Tony Robbins quote. AZ Quotes. (n.d.). Retrieved March 30, 2022, from https://www.azquotes.com/quote/1457094

Townley, C. (2006). *Houseworks*. Dorling Kindersley. p. 14.

Vision quotes. Brainy Quote. (n.d.). Retrieved March 31, 2022 from https://www.brainyquote.com/topics/vision-quotes

Vision quotes. Goodreads. (n.d.). Retrieved March 31, 2022 from https://www.goodreads.com/quotes/tag/vision

www.ingramcontent.com/pod-product-compliance
Lightning Source LLC
Chambersburg PA
CBHW030253100526
44590CB00012B/382